DailyOM
LEARNING
TO LIVE

ALSO BY MADISYN TAYLOR

DailyOM: Inspirational Thoughts for a Happy, Healthy, and Fulfilling Day

HAY HOUSE TITLES OF RELATED INTEREST

YOU CAN HEAL YOUR LIFE, the movie,
starring Louise L. Hay & Friends
(available as a 1-DVD program and an expanded 2-DVD set)
Watch the trailer at: **www.LouiseHayMovie.com**

THE SHIFT, the movie, starring Dr. Wayne W. Dyer
(available as a 1-DVD program and an expanded 2-DVD set)
Watch the trailer at: **www.DyerMovie.com**

৽৽৽

THE ART OF EXTREME SELF-CARE:
Transform Your Life One Month at a Time, by Cheryl Richardson

AWAKENING TO THE SECRET CODE OF YOUR MIND:
Your Mind's Journey to Inner Peace, by Dr. Darren R. Weissman

COMMUNICATION WITH ALL LIFE:
Revelations of an Animal Communicator, by Joan Ranquet

A DAILY DOSE OF SANITY: A Five-Minute
Soul Recharge for Every Day of the Year, by Alan Cohen

DAILY GUIDANCE FROM YOUR ANGELS: 365 Angelic
Messages to Soothe, Heal, and Open Your Heart, by Doreen Virtue

HEALING YOUR FAMILY HISTORY: 5 Steps to
Break Free of Destructive Patterns, by Rebecca Linder Hintze

IT'S NOT THE END OF THE WORLD: Developing
Resilience in Times of Change, by Joan Borysenko, Ph.D.

VITAMINS FOR THE SOUL: Daily Doses of Wisdom
for Personal Empowerment, by Sonia Choquette

WAITING FOR AUTUMN, by Scott Blum

৽৽৽

All of the above are available at your local bookstore,
or may be ordered by visiting:

Hay House USA: **www.hayhouse.com**®
Hay House Australia: **www.hayhouse.com.au**
Hay House UK: **www.hayhouse.co.uk**
Hay House South Africa: **www.hayhouse.co.za**
Hay House India: **www.hayhouse.co.in**

DailyOM
LEARNING
TO LIVE

MADISYN TAYLOR

HAY HOUSE, INC.
Carlsbad, California • New York City
London • Sydney • Johannesburg
Vancouver • Hong Kong • New Delhi

Published and distributed in the United States by: Hay House, Inc.: www
.hayhouse.com • *Published and distributed in Australia by:* Hay House
Australia Pty. Ltd.: www.hayhouse.com.au • *Published and distributed
in the United Kingdom by:* Hay House UK, Ltd.: www.hayhouse.co.uk
• *Published and distributed in the Republic of South Africa by:* Hay
House SA (Pty), Ltd.: www.hayhouse.co.za • *Distributed in Canada
by:* Raincoast: www.raincoast.com • *Published in India by:* Hay House
Publishers India: www.hayhouse.co.in

Design: Nick C. Welch

Library of Congress Cataloging-in-Publication Data

Taylor, Madisyn.
  DailyOM : learning to live / Madisyn Taylor. -- 1st ed.
    p. cm.
  ISBN 978-1-4019-2558-1 (hbk. : alk. paper) 1. Mind and body. 2.
Consciousness. 3. Self. I. Title.
  BF161.T237 2010
  158.1'28--dc22

                                    2009012957

ISBN: 978-1-4019-2558-1

13 12 11 10   4 3 2 1/
1st edition, February 2010

Printed in the United States of America

CONTENTS

PREFACE

I've often wished people were born with instruction manuals. Each would be different based on what we needed to learn, but the basics would be the same: how to create healthy relationships, how to deal with sorrow and pain, how to reach our goals, and how to know what we want to do with our lives when we grow up. We'd continue to have our own unique life lessons, but we'd have a guide to refer to when we were feeling overwhelmed or lost.

In real life, we don't come with such a manual—or a warranty registration card, for that matter—to help fix us when we feel broken. What I've done with this book is the next best thing to a manual. I've set up tools so that you can actually learn to live your life in accordance with what your soul desires . . . learning to live the life you were meant to and having a guardian angel in the form of a book to help you along the way. We weren't meant to go through life completely lost, without help, and I believe it's part of my soul's purpose to help people navigate their own lives.

It is one of my greatest blessings to be able to use my work as a vehicle to help others. In March of 2004, my husband and I started a company called DailyOM, which sends out free inspirational e-mails each weekday to our subscribers. Every day a message of hope, inspiration, peace, and healing is circulated out into the world as it makes its rounds among e-mail in-boxes across our great earth. The natural progression of this led me to put out my first book, *DailyOM: Inspirational Thoughts for a Happy, Healthy, and Fulfilling Day* (Hay House, 2008), which was so well received that a second one was called for.

This new book is formatted slightly differently. It's divided into nine basic parts, starting out with *Being Honest with Yourself* and ending with *Helping Others.* In between is a magnificent journey of DailyOM stories—along with those from my own life so that you can read about times when I've been in the very same place you may be in, whether that place is one of feeling lost or confused or even at the point of giving up all hope of being happy. An amazing life is waiting for you. Your life.

INTRODUCTION

When I started to talk with people about my first book, I noticed a pattern of frequently asked questions, the most common being: "How do you come up with a new DailyOM idea every day?" I sometimes wonder myself as I look back on the years without having ever missed a deadline. It became apparent soon after DailyOM was launched that I was to use my life experiences to help others. This gave me great relief, because it seemed a shame to have gone through so much pain, heartache, and growth just for myself without being able to share what I'd gained with others. It almost seemed wasted on one person. I've always been an open book and happy to share what I've learned with others so that their own journeys may be easier.

Soon I developed a system of working with the universe to help fine-tune the DailyOM stories. I decided to pick one day a week when I wouldn't go into the office and would instead stay home and have a meditation day. I picked Tuesday for no particular reason.

First thing in the morning I sit at my altar and just spend some time there, clearing my head, breathing, and lighting a candle and incense. I then set my intention that this time be for writing down story ideas (five of them at a sitting) and ask to be a clear channel to receive the wisdom of the universe. At that point either I'm left completely blank or the messages start coming in strong. I'm shown an event or circumstance in my life and start to write down notes. I then feel what it was like to be in that situation, what I went through, the steps I took, and how I healed and moved on. This process usually leaves me with about a paragraph of notes containing the essence of the story, although an entire story has come through all at once before.

Often I'm asked to go outside, and I always love it when this guidance comes because of my enjoyment of nature and her profound messages. I may feel guided to watch ants or commune with a tree, and I know that a beautiful metaphorical story about nature and humanity will come forth. These are some of my very favorite stories because they're easy for all to access and understand, as they're very disarming to the soul.

The next logical question people always ask me is: "Do you mind being used in this way?" I don't feel "used" at all, although sometimes I'd like a break from the lessons that seem to come every single day. I feel that this is a commitment I made on a soul level, and in return the universe provides for me and I am never without what I need. This work is in me, and even if I wanted to, I couldn't escape it. When I receive e-mails from readers about how these stories have changed their lives, I'm brought to my knees in tears of gratitude. There's no greater feeling to me than fulfilling my life's purpose and doing what elevates my soul, what makes it sing.

You too have the ability to allow your own soul to sing, and like me, you may find it takes a while to learn what it is that makes you happy and fulfilled. The journey is so worth it, and on those days when you just feel like giving up, take a deep breath and know that you are not alone.

Blessings,
Madisyn

PART I
BEING HONEST WITH YOURSELF

 don't think we can fully heal ourselves unless we begin to be honest with ourselves. We tend to think that's what we're doing, but in reality most of us aren't being honest and authentic at all. When we aren't honest within *ourselves,* how we can be fully honest and present for others? It's as if we're giving them the bits that we want them to see, the bits that we like and feel are worthy of others. We can even fool ourselves into believing that we're a certain way and presenting it to the world, when in fact we're experiencing feelings of deep shame, insignificance, and not being good enough. We justify it by reasoning that if we don't acknowledge all aspects of our being, then surely the bad bits will go away, or we can keep them hidden and under cover.

Everybody wants to present their best side to the world—that's part of being human. But eventually this wears down and becomes a burden and a sham. I find that when I'm honest with myself, it becomes so much easier to be honest with others . . . and to my surprise, it seems to have the effect of their loving me even more for my honesty. My friends now embrace my good, bad, and ugly bits because *I* do. We don't realize the burden and weight we carry when we're not forthright with ourselves.

Try to pick one trait of yours that you're not being truthful about and let it come to the surface—don't allow it to hide anymore. Allow your friends and family to be exposed to it and talk about it. You may be surprised by their reaction, and because of your honesty, you may even allow them to reveal more of *their* authentic selves by being brave enough to do it first.

❧

When I started to do press for my first book, I can honestly say I wasn't looking forward to it. I was scared that people wouldn't like me or take me seriously; I was scared I'd say the wrong thing, or worse yet, completely blank out. I'd purposely stayed hidden for a long time, working anonymously for years with my writing just to avoid being in the public eye, for fear of ridicule.

Before my first radio interview I paced the floor, secretly hoping the station would call and cancel it. I changed my shirt twice because I was perspiring so much. The call came and I was on the air. Yes, I was nervous at first, but my hosts put me at ease. Next thing I knew, it was over: 20 minutes had flown by, and I was on a high afterward—I wanted to do it again! I realized at that point that sometimes I mix up the feelings of being scared and being excited. If you've ever had to perform onstage, you know the sensation of butterflies beforehand, but then once your performance starts, you're simply flowing in the moment.

Eventually some things that I feared about my press tour did happen, including the time when I was talking and then completely lost my train of thought. I was just honest with the host and started to laugh, telling him that I completely forgot what I wanted to say. It was a recorded show, and I asked if he could take that part out. He said he didn't want to because it showed how real I was. We ended up having a good laugh about it together.

A wonderful friend once told me that anything worth doing will have some fear attached to it. When I think about all of the things I've done in my life that have brought on the feeling of being scared, they were the ones I needed to accomplish to get over a hurdle and move to the next level or stage of my life. If it were easy, then there would really be no point, no learning. Many of my lessons are filled with both fear and excitement; it's a bit like getting on a plane and having a fear of flying but knowing I'm going somewhere tropical, which is the exciting part.

❦

In a complete effort to try to be honest with myself, somewhere along my healing journey, I got stuck. I imagine it's something like what a person on a diet goes through, reaching a plateau and then not losing any more weight. For me it came in the form of a full and sudden halt in my healing process. I found that I could make a big dent in some of my issues, but then progress would stop, almost as if I were putting the brakes on.

I've begun to recognize when I participate in self-sabotage, and I believe I'm a master at that, but this feeling was different. In order to discover what was going on, I had to go into deep meditation and feel around a bit. In this process, I found that there was a part of me that didn't want to heal.

Although it sounds counterintuitive, it made perfect sense. We all have a part of ourselves that is scared, because when we heal, we grow and our hearts open more, and this can make us feel vulnerable. The part of ourselves that is scared and wants to keep us down isn't sabotaging; it is simply protecting us from pain—it's doing its job and doing it well. This part of us can be scared for so many different reasons. For me it meant that I would have to go out and face the world and let people know how I feel and what I've learned, thus opening myself up to ridicule.

The part of me that didn't want to heal would keep me home in the form of depression, sickness, and fear of public spaces (agoraphobia). My whole world opened up when I realized what was going on—I wasn't broken, I wasn't crazy, and I wasn't inadequate. I always say that the first step to change is realization and awareness, and now *I* had a profound realization that energized me, and I could use it as a tool to help myself. By starting a conversation with this part of myself that wanted to stay hidden and safe, I was able to make it feel comfortable enough to welcome change.

LOVE OR FEAR
WHERE WE ARE COMING FROM

Whether our actions are motivated by fear or love is a classic question of spiritual inquiry. In this line of thinking, it is not what we do that is of paramount importance, but rather the feeling *behind* what we do. For example, we might pursue a particular type of work out of a fear of poverty; or, alternatively, we might pursue it from a place of loving the work itself. We all know from experience that doing something out of love is qualitatively different from doing the same thing out of fear. Most of us have a balance of the two motivations playing out in our lives, and it can be an interesting experiment to observe ourselves, attempting to notice where most of our motivation comes from.

The majority of us fear a run-in with the law, and consciously or unconsciously, we avoid actions that might create that situation. So it is natural to do some things out of fear. However, we could also avoid breaking the law out of love for ourselves and the people who depend on us. This is just changing the way we think about things by examining the matter from a different angle, and sometimes that is all that is required to change our experience.

If, in the course of our self-examination, we find a great many fear-based actions, we can probably find ways in which they might actually stem from love. For example, instead of thinking that we are working at a job because we fear for our family's survival, we might see that we are doing so because we love our family and this is the best way to support them. Just this simple shift, from working out of fear to working from a place of love, can have the effect of altering our existence without requiring us to change anything.

❧

LIFE AS WE KNOW IT
THE STATUS QUO

When our lives are going well, and sometimes even when they are not, we may find ourselves feeling very attached to the status quo of our existence—life as we know it. It is a very human tendency to resist change as if it were possible to simply *decide* not to do it or have it in our lives. But change will come and the status quo will go . . . sooner or later, with our consent or without it. We may find at the end of the day that we feel considerably more empowered when we find the courage to ally ourselves with the universal force of change, rather than working against it.

Of course, the answer is not to go about changing things at random, without regard to whether they are working or not. There is a time and place for stability and the preservation of what has been gained over time. In fact, the ability to stabilize and preserve what is serving us is part of what helps us survive and thrive. The problem comes when we become more attached to preserving the status quo than to honoring the universal givens of growth and change. For example, if we allow a situation we are in to remain stagnant simply because we are comfortable, it may be time for us to summon up the courage to challenge the status quo.

This may be painful at times or surprisingly liberating, and it will most likely be a little of both. Underneath the discomfort, we will probably find excitement and energy as we take the risk of unblocking the natural flow of energy in our lives. It is like dismantling a dam inside ourselves, because most of the work involves clearing our own inner obstacles so that the river of our life can flow unobstructed. Once we remove the obstacles, we can simply go with the flow, trusting the changes that follow.

MOVING BEYOND DEFINITIONS
OVERIDENTIFYING WITH LABELS

As humans, we possess the tendency to name and categorize things. This applies to everything from plants and animals to styles to ourselves and others. Everyone who walks the earth carries or has carried some label—such as *white, old, artist, animal lover, parent, child,* or *liberal*—which either they themselves or others used to define them. While labels can help us form useful first impressions, they can also act as a thick filter between us and the world. Expectations are derived from labels. When we begin to define others in terms of their profession, looks, wealth, or political background, it becomes harder to accept them unconditionally. And when we define who we are with strict labels, we limit ourselves and our potential by effectively pigeonholing our identities. The challenge lies in finding a balance between that which defines us and our evolving natures.

We first learn who we are when we are children. Identity is forged by society, which labels us so-and-so's child, a boy or a girl, a reader or a jock, or a shy or outgoing person. This is natural, considering that characterizing others upon first meeting is an automatic process. But when we regard these initial impressions as unchangeable, we deny the fact that we are all blessed with roles that can change from one day to the next or exist simultaneously with other roles. It is possible to be both a parent and an artist, and a runner and a businesswoman.

If you were to choose a single role, such as artist, it would limit the paths you could take. If you were, however, to say, "I am a creative person, although that creativity is sometimes blocked," it would open new avenues of exploration because you could express your creativity in many ways.

People are so much more than what they do or have done, and all are potentially capable of taking on a new identity or letting go of an old one because of emotional or environmental factors. You may choose to be "a strong-willed executive" at one moment and "a nurturing parent" at another. Yet you remain wholly you.

Although labels can be a good stepping-off point, they are no substitute for understanding who we really are. If everyone was encouraged to look beyond labels, open-mindedness and tolerance would be the inevitable result.

SHEDDING LIGHT ON OURSELVES
PARTS THAT DO NOT WANT TO HEAL

In almost every case, we know what is best for us in our lives, from the relationships we create to the food we eat. Still, somewhat mysteriously, it is often difficult to make the right choices for ourselves. We find ourselves hanging out with someone who leaves us feeling drained, or choosing to eat fast food over a salad. We go through phases where we stop practicing yoga or taking vitamins, even though we feel so much better when we do these things. Often we have no idea why we continue to make the less-enlightened choice, but it is important that we search within ourselves to find out.

When we choose that which is not best for us, the truth can be that there is a deep-seated part of us that does not want to heal. We may say it is because we do not have the time or the energy or the resources, but the real truth is that when we do not take care of ourselves, we are falling prey to self-sabotage. Self-sabotage happens unconsciously, which is why it is so difficult to see that we are doing it. The important thing to realize is that this part of us that resists our healing is the very one that most needs our attention and love. Even as it appears to be working against us, if we can simply bring it into the light of our consciousness, it can become our greatest ally. It carries the information we need to move to the next level in our healing process.

When we recognize that we are not making healthy choices, we might even say out loud, "I am not taking care of myself." Sometimes this is the jolt we need to wake up to what is actually happening. Next, we can sit ourselves down in meditation, with a journal, or with a trusted friend to explore the matter more thoroughly. Just shining the light of our awareness on the source of our resistance is sometimes enough to dispel its power. At other times, further effort is required. Either way, we need not fear these parts that do not want to heal. We only need to take them under our wing and bring them with us into the light.

CAUSE, EFFECT, AND TRANSFORMATION
FEELING DEPLETED

There are times in our lives when it seems our bodies are running on empty. We are not sick, nor are we necessarily pushing ourselves to the limit—rather, the energy we typically enjoy has mysteriously dissipated, leaving only fatigue. Many people grow accustomed to feeling this way because they do not know that it is possible to exist in any other state. The body's natural state, however, is one of energy, clarity, and balance. Cultivating these virtues in our own bodies so that we can combat feelings of depletion is a matter of developing a refined awareness of the self and then making changes based on our observations.

A few scant moments of focused self-examination in which you assess your recent schedule, diet, and general health may help you zero in on the factors causing your depletion. If you are struggling to cope with an overly full agenda, prioritization can provide you with more time to sleep and otherwise refresh yourself. Switching to a diet containing plenty of nutritious foods may serve to restore your vigor, especially when augmented by supplements like B vitamins or ginseng. Consider, too, that a visit to a healer or homeopath will likely provide you with wonderful insights into your tiredness.

But identifying the source of your exhaustion will occasionally be more complicated than spotting a void in your lifestyle and filling it with some form of literal nourishment. Since your earthly and ethereal forms are so intimately entwined, matters of the mind and heart can take their toll on your physical self. Intense emotions such as anger, sadness, jealousy, and regret need fuel to manifest in your consciousness; and this fuel is more often than not bodily energy. Conversely, a lack of mental and emotional stimulation may leave you feeling listless and lethargic.

Coping with and healing physical depletion will be easier when you accept that the underlying cause might be more complex than you at first imagined. A harried lifestyle or a diet low in vital nutrients can represent only one part of a larger issue affecting your mood, stamina, and energy levels. When you believe that you are ultimately in control of how you feel, you will be empowered to transform yourself and your day-to-day life so that fatigue can no longer gain a lasting foothold in your existence.

NO WRONG RESPONSE
EXPERIENCES SHAPE YOUR REACTIONS

Our view of the universe is largely determined by our experiences. It is when we are caught off guard by the spontaneity of existence that we are most apt to respond authentically, even when our feelings do not correspond with those of the multitude. Events that arouse strong emotions within us or are surprising in nature can be disquieting, for often it is in their aftermath that we discover how profoundly our histories have shaped us. The differences that divide us from our peers are highlighted in our reactions when these diverge from the mainstream, and this can be highly upsetting because it forces us to confront the uniqueness of our lives.

When our response to unexpected news or startling ideas is not the same as that of the people around us, we may feel driven by a desire to dismiss our feelings as irrational or incorrect. But reactions themselves are neither right nor wrong. The forces that sculpted the patterns that to a large extent dictate *our* development are not the same forces that shaped the development of our relatives, friends, colleagues, or neighbors. There is no reason to believe that one person's reaction to a particular event is somehow more valid than another's. How we respond to the constant changes taking place in the world around us is a product of our history, a testament to our individuality, and a part of the healing process that allows us to address key elements of our past in a context we can grasp in the present.

Life's pivotal events can provide you with a way to define yourself as a unique and matchless being, but you must put aside the judgments that might otherwise prevent you from gaining insight into your distinct mode of interpreting the world. Try to internalize your feelings without categorizing or evaluating them. When you feel unsure of the legitimacy of your reactions, remember that cultural, sociological, spiritual, and familial differences can cause two people to interpret a single event in widely dissimilar ways. Examining your responses outside of the context provided by others can show you that your emotional complexity is something to be valued, for it has made you who you are today.

TRANSLATING YOUR FEELINGS
ARE YOU EXCITED OR SCARED?

When new challenges and opportunities show up in our lives, we may diagnose ourselves as feeling scared when what we really feel is excited. Often we have not been taught how to welcome the thrill of a new opportunity, so we opt to back off, indulging our anxiety instead of awakening our courage. One way to inspire ourselves to embrace the opportunities that come our way is to look more deeply into our feelings and see that butterflies in the stomach and a rapidly beating heart are not necessarily signs that we are afraid. Those very same feelings can be translated as excitement, curiosity, passion, and even love.

There is nothing wrong with being afraid as long as we do not let it stop us from doing the things that excite us. Most of us assume that brave people are fearless, but the truth is that they are simply more comfortable with fear because they face it on a regular basis. The more we do this, the more we feel excitement in the face of challenges rather than anxiety. The more we cultivate our ability to move forward instead of backing off, the more we trust ourselves to handle the new opportunity—whether it is a job, an exciting move, or a relationship. When we feel our fear, we can remind ourselves that maybe we are actually just excited. We can assure ourselves that this opportunity has come our way because we are meant to take it.

Framing things just a little differently can dramatically shift our mental state from one of resistance to one of openness. We can practice this new way of seeing things by saying aloud: "I am really excited about this job interview," "I am really looking forward to going on a date with this amazing person," or "I am excited to have the opportunity to do something I have never done before." As we do so, we will feel our energy shift from fear, which paralyzes, to excitement, which empowers us to direct all that energy in the service of moving forward, growing, and learning.

❦

UNBLOCKING THE ALLY
HABITUAL ANGER

Sometimes when we feel anger, it is coming from a deep place that demands acknowledgment and expression. At these times, it is important that we find healthy ways to honor it, remembering how dangerous it is to repress it. However, anger can also become a habit, our go-to emotion whenever things go wrong. Often this is because, for whatever reason, we feel more comfortable expressing it than we do other emotions, like sadness. It can also be that getting mad gives us the impression that we have done something about our problem. In these cases, our habitual anger is inhibiting our ability both to express our other emotions and to take action in our lives.

If it is true that anger is functioning this way in your life, the first thing you might want to try is to notice when you experience it. You may begin to see a pattern of some kind. For example, you could notice that it is always your first response, or that it comes up a lot in one particular situation. If the pattern does not become clear right away, you could try keeping a journal about when you get angry and see if you can find any underlying meaning. The good thing about a journal is that you can explore your anger more deeply in it—from examining who in your family of origin expressed a lot of rage to noting how you feel when you encounter this emotion in others. This kind of awareness can be a formidable agent of transformation.

Anger can be a powerful ally, since it is filled with energy that we can harness and use to create change in the world. It is one of the most cathartic emotions, and it can also be a very effective cleanser of the emotional system. However, when it becomes a habit, it actually loses its power to transform and becomes an obstacle to growth. Identifying the role anger plays in your life and restoring it to its proper function can bring new energy and expansiveness to your emotional life.

❦

BEYOND BEHAVIOR
DEFENSE MECHANISMS

We all have defense mechanisms that we have developed over time, often without being aware of it. In times of trouble, the behaviors that have worked to get us past challenges with the least amount of pain are the ones that we repeat . . . even when part of us knows they no longer work. Such behavior is a natural response from the mental and physical aspects of our being. But because we are spiritual beings as well, we have the ability to rise above habits and patterns to see the truth that lies beyond. And from that moment on, we can make choices that allow us to work directly from that place of truth within us.

Most of our defense mechanisms were developed in childhood—from the moment we realized crying would get us the attention we craved. Passive-aggressive ways of communicating may have allowed us to obtain what we needed without being scolded, punished, or laughed at, so we learned to avoid being direct and honest. Some of us may have taken refuge in the lives of others, discovering ways to divert attention away from ourselves entirely. Throwing ourselves into projects or rescuing others from themselves can be effective ways to avoid dealing with our own issues. And when people are truly helped by our actions, we get the added bonus of feeling heroic. But while defenses can keep away the things we fear, they can also work to keep our good from us.

When we can be honest with ourselves about what we truly desire, then we can connect our desires to the creative power of the spirit within us. Knowing that we are one with the energy of the universe allows us to release any need for defense. Trusting that power, we know that we are exactly where we are meant to be, and that challenges bring gifts of growth and experience. When we can put down arms raised in defense, then we are free to use our hands, minds, hearts, and spirits to mold and shape our abundant energy to create and live our lives.

❦

A MATTER OF SIGNIFICANCE
RECOGNIZING YOUR VALUE

It can be easy sometimes to buy into the illusion of our own insignificance. We may see large corporations or institutions, celebrities, or successful people in our community and compare ourselves to them, thinking that their material power or fame affirms how little our own lives amount to. But nothing could be further from the truth. Every single one of us matters—tremendously. Our very existence affects countless people in countless ways. And because we are each essentially a microcosm of the larger universe, our internal experiences affect the whole of life more than we could ever imagine. The world simply could not exist as it does now if you, or any one of us, were not in it.

Perhaps you are aware that on some level you believe your life does not matter. If this thought resonates within you, maybe it is time to explore why you feel this way. You may have formed self-rejecting or belittling beliefs as a child to keep yourself safe or to help make sense of confusing situations. You may have felt unseen or unheard and decided that there was something wrong with you, rather than with the attention span of the people around you. Spend some time looking into where these feelings of insignificance first took root, and see what changes you might be able to make in your life and in your heart.

This one belief in your own unimportance could be limiting you and affecting your life in enormous ways. When you shift your perceptions around your own ability to affect your life and impact the world, you may discover wonderful parts of yourself that you had long ago forgotten. There may even be exciting new parts that you never knew existed. When you gain awareness of how much your life really does matter, fresh sources of energy can emerge and your sense of connection with the world is renewed.

❦

HOVERING AROUND THE SUN
AVOIDING THE CENTER

It is funny to imagine our lives as things we spend a lot of time avoiding, because it seems like that would be impossible to do. Our lives consist of everything we engage in, from showering to sleeping, but also a lot of busywork that distracts us and keeps us from looking within. Experiencing life from the inside means taking time each day to simply be alone and quiet in the presence of our souls. Many of us are so out of practice that it is almost unnerving to have a moment to ourselves. As a result, we may have stopped trying to carve out that time to take a seat at the center of our lives.

One of the reasons why it can be uncomfortable to sit with ourselves is because when we do, we tend to open ourselves to an inner voice, which might question the way we are living or some of the choices we are making. Sometimes the voice reminds us of our secret, inner yearnings—dreams we thought we had forgotten. When we already feel overwhelmed by our busy schedules, the idea of hearing this voice can sound exhausting. However, its reflections are the cords that connect us to our authentic selves, and they are the very things that make life worth living. When we continually avoid connecting with our lives, we risk losing out on the very purpose of our existence.

To begin the process of being more present and less absent in your life, you might want to set aside just a few minutes each day to simply sit with yourself. This does not mean watching a movie or reading a book, but taking time daily for self-examination in order to avoid the avoidance— to be with yourself in an open way. After a while, you may start to enjoy this part of the day so much that you make less busywork for yourself so that you can spend more time at the center of your own life, rather than hovering like a planet around the sun.

❦

PART II
ACCEPTING THE LIFE YOU CREATE

Have you ever witnessed others living lives different from your own . . . people who are perhaps paralyzed, have lost limbs, or are in a wheelchair? The first reaction is to feel sorry for them and wonder how they get through the day living as they do. If you were to speak to these individuals, they probably would surprise you with their upbeat attitude and how they've learned to cope and manage their lives.

I'd like to introduce you to the concept that these people have *chosen* these lives for themselves, more than likely before they were even born. Again, a first reaction to this reasoning would be: *Nobody would <u>choose</u> to live with an illness or disability!* But, you see, it is your thinking mind and your ego that are feeling this way. Your soul self doesn't view it in the same way at all. It is so pure and wants to learn and evolve, so it maps out a plan for your life to include hardships, tough times, and a dark night of the soul so that it may learn and grow.

When I look back on my childhood, I remember a frightened little girl growing up in a household that was filled with dysfunction, rage, and mental abuse. I was so sensitive and frightened that I built a "room within" my bedroom that was inside my closet, where I felt safe. I began having panic attacks at a very early age and suicidal thoughts as I went through high school. I grew up feeling very unloved and was constantly in protection/survival mode. When I look back on that sweet little girl, I could just weep for her; I want to sweep her into my arms and hold her and tell her that she is loved and that all will be okay.

Now, as an adult and after spending many years working on my issues to become a more aware person, I realize that if I hadn't had that particular experience as a child, I wouldn't be the person I am today; I wouldn't be doing the work I'm doing today. There will always be a part of me that grieves not feeling loved as a little girl, but I know in my heart that it's what my soul wanted—that my soul knew I could heal enough from those wounds to go forth in the world and live a loving life.

~~~

In recent years it has become a popular belief that we must always have positive thoughts—that what we think, we attract. This is true, but it's also important to know that thoughts can't be simply stuffed away or always made into something positive. It is normal human behavior to have unwanted thoughts, and this occurs more when we're experiencing stress or anxiety.

I had an experience once where I was able to witness firsthand in real time the effect of thoughts. My house had been damaged by a bad rainstorm—my guest-room ceiling was about to collapse, and the wood floors were ruined. I called up my insurance company, and they sent out a field representative to survey the damage. As this man was getting ready to give me his report, I felt a shift in his energy, and I knew bad news was coming: they wouldn't give me money for the repairs.

Ordinarily I would have one of two reactions: The first would be to come out fighting and give the speech about how I'd been paying premiums for 20 years and had multiple policies with the company and would now change insurance carriers. The second route would be to simply avoid the situation and accept his answer and then just sit and stew in my anger. In that instant, before the words could come out of the man's mouth, I made the decision that I would not react and go to the "bad place"; I would listen to what he was going to tell me and assume that all would be well.

The most amazing thing happened as soon as I had that thought. Before the man could start to utter anything negative about not paying my claim, he stopped and asked me to wait a moment. He then made a phone call, had a conversation about insurance and construction, and hung up. A smile spread across his face, and he said, "Good news— I can write you a check!"

I will never truly know whether my thoughts actually averted a potential negative outcome, because a lot of times things *don't* go my way or how I'd envisioned. During these times I've learned to trust the universe, and more often than not, at some point I realize that it never lets me down.

This is part of the process of learning to accept the life you're given, and when this state is reached, you will truly be in the flow.

❦

FOCUSING ON THE BEST YOU
COMPARING YOURSELF TO OTHERS

Each of us has been blessed with unique qualities. No one else has lived through precisely the same circumstances, possesses exactly the same traits, or thinks just the same thoughts. We love, appreciate, and hold dear vastly different things. Because of this, it is nearly impossible to justifiably compare oneself to others, yet so many people stake their happiness on how they fare when measured against a neighbor, co-worker, sibling, or Hollywood star.

It is easy to think that if you had "her" eyes, "his" house, "her" job, or "his" money, you would be truly happy. Your value as a person has little to do with what you look like or possess, and comparing yourself to someone else denies your own wonderful gifts and talents. Everyone has value, but the source of this value is individual. Learning to stop comparing yourself to others begins with accepting your own worth, because *self*-acceptance is the most important thing.

Regularly assessing your worth in terms of other people's gifts—be they talent, money, looks, or material wealth—can lead to dissatisfaction even when you are on top of your game. It is important to remember that you are *you* and will always be you, not someone else. Your individuality is something to take pride in. When you get the urge to compare yourself to someone else, meditate on the fact that you are lovable, capable, and special the way you are. Instead of focusing on traits you do not possess and others do, concentrate on what you yourself have. You may be artistic, very funny, or physically fit. Or you may be exceptionally organized, a capable parent, or profoundly patient. Usually when we compare ourselves to others, we come out feeling devalued.

The gifts you have been given can be used for the benefit of everyone you come into contact with. Realizing and embracing such a concept enables you to focus on bringing out the best in yourself so that you can celebrate your own achievements as well as those of others.

❦

CONTROLLING YOUR MIND
UNWANTED THOUGHTS

Negative thoughts exist for all of humankind. When they arise, they can spiral into a deluge of gloomy reflections or even depression. There are times when it seems impossible to stop thinking of the world's ills or replaying every moment of a bad memory. It is like having a song stuck in your head, only more intense and emotionally draining. Unwanted thoughts that persist can distract you from your life. Luckily, there are ways to consciously release these thoughts and to trick your mind into refocusing its attention on more positive subjects.

When unwanted, dark thoughts are swirling in your head, it can be difficult to concentrate on anything else. You need to take back your attention and refocus it. Start by shouting out loud—or inside your mind—something jarring and to the point, such as "Stop!" or "That's enough!" Any word or phrase is fine as long as it is momentarily shocking.

This may be enough, or you may want to try *thought stopping*. First, take a few deep breaths; relax; and picture a scene in which you feel comfortable, optimistic, and good about yourself. Note every detail, even if the setting is not a real place. The next time unwanted thoughts occur, yell "Stop!" and then immediately begin imagining your scene, replacing the unwanted thought with something positive.

Never try to "think away" an unwanted thought because you will simply strengthen it. It can be helpful to share your concern with someone, thereby lessening your mind's preoccupation with it. If you are uncomfortable doing so, simply distract yourself when intrusive thoughts begin cycling. Recite the alphabet, tackle some chores, do a puzzle, exercise (which releases hormones that may quell negative thinking), or perform a conscious-breathing meditation.

It is natural to experience unpleasant thought patterns or even obsess over a memory, but there is no need to let it overwhelm you. It may be difficult at first to replace negative thoughts with positive ones or to concentrate on a puzzle when you cannot let go of something. Techniques like thought stopping and using other forms of distraction to rid yourself of unwelcome thoughts get easier and easier with time, and they really do work.

IT BEGINS WITH YOU
LEARNING TO LOVE YOURSELF

We have all heard it countless times before: "To experience true love, we first must love ourselves," or some such variation. However it is stated, the importance of self-love is vital to becoming a healthy, whole human being. We are all children of the universe, created out of love. We accept and love other people, animals, nature . . . all that comes from the same source we do. We too, then, are worthy of our own love. To honor oneself with caring and acceptance is to honor the universe that created us.

Self-love is about fully embracing ourselves, realizing our strengths and accepting our flaws. It is not about being self-centered or self-absorbed, which is based on insecurity and not knowing ourselves. True self-love is a guarantee that we will not succumb to such selfish pursuits. For if we truly love ourselves, we know that we do not need to be the best looking or most talented or have the most possessions. When we love ourselves, we are able to give love freely to others without fear of being hurt or used. We love ourselves enough not to allow others to take advantage of us. And when we are secure in our love of self, we attract the love of others.

To learn to love yourself, treat yourself the way you treat those you care about. Be kind to yourself, giving yourself all you need to be happy and healthy. Show yourself a good time by doing things you like. Eat well and take care of your body. Say nice things to yourself. Compliment and praise yourself, just as you would a friend, family member, or lover. Encourage yourself when you are feeling down.

And most important, say the words that we all long to hear. Look in the mirror and tell yourself, "I love you." This can be difficult, but it is a powerful tool in acceptance and self-love. It may not be easy—you may feel foolish at first—but you can do it. Even if you do not feel it right away, keep doing it. Love yourself first, and you will be able to truly love others and to *be* truly loved in return.

❦

STRONGER THAN YOU KNOW
GETTING ALL WORKED UP

Our power to cope successfully with life's challenges far outstrips our capacity for feeling nervous. Yet in the weeks, days, and hours leading up to an event we believe will test the limits of our abilities, the opposite often seems true. While we may have previously regarded ourselves as equal to the trials that lie ahead, we reach a point at which they seem perilously near, and our anxiety begins to mount. We then become increasingly worked up, until the moment of truth arrives and we discover that our worry was for naught.

We are almost always stronger and more capable than we believe ourselves to be. But anxiety is not rational in nature, which means that in most cases we cannot work through it using logic as our only tool. Reason can help us recognize the relative futility of unwarranted worry, but more often than not we will find a more potent source of comfort in patterns of thought and activity that redirect our attention to practical or engaging matters.

Most of us find it remarkably difficult to focus on two distinct thoughts or emotions at once, and we can use this natural human limitation to our advantage when trying to stay centered in the period leading up to a potentially tricky or taxing experience. When we concentrate on something unrelated to our worry—such as deep breathing, visualizations of success, demanding yet pleasurable pursuits, or exercise—anxiety dissipates naturally. If we focus on preparing ourselves for every possible contingency, distraction becomes practical because our preparations serve both to eliminate potential causes of anxiety and to prove that the worst outcome we can imagine is seldom *that* bad. Meditation is also a useful coping mechanism, as it provides us with a means to ground ourselves in the moment. Our guides can aid us by providing us with a focal point wholly outside of our own sphere.

The intense emotional flare-up you experience just before you are set to challenge yourself is often a mixture of both excitement and fear. When you take steps to eliminate the latter, you can more fully enjoy the former. Although you may find it difficult to avoid getting worked up, your awareness of the forces acting on your feelings will help you return to your center and accept that few hurdles you face will be as high as they at first appear.

❦

YOU ARE BEAUTIFUL
SEEING YOURSELF

Many of us do not take the time to notice and acknowledge how beautiful we are as human beings. We may be great lovers of beauty, seeing it in the people, places, and things around us, while completely missing it in ourselves. Some of us feel that it is vain to consider our appearance too much, or we may find that when we look at ourselves, all we see are imperfections. Often we look in the mirror with expectations and preconceived notions that blind us from seeing ourselves clearly. As a result, we miss the beauty that is closest to us, the beauty we are. Sometimes we see beauty in a shallow way, noticing how well we are conforming to social norms, but failing to see the deeper kind that shines out from within and will continue to do so regardless of how we measure up to society's ideals.

If we can cut through all these obstacles and simply appreciate how beautiful we are, we free up so much energy. We also become less dependent upon the opinions and feedback of others since we become our own greatest admirers. Many of us know that after a great yoga practice or a long, deep meditation, we are better able to see how beautiful we are. This is because we have released some of our baggage, thus unburdening ourselves and summoning forth the spirit that dwells within us. It is the heady combination of the divine spirit and the human body that conveys beauty more accurately than anything else.

To keep ourselves in touch with our own beauty, we can surround ourselves with images that reflect it back to us—photos of a relative who has our eyes, images of teachers who embody the same spirit, or self-portraits that capture our essence in a way that allows us to see ourselves anew. The best way to stay in touch with our beauty is to keep looking deeply into our own souls and opening our eyes to the human beings we see in the mirror every day.

❧

NOTHING BIG REQUIRED
YOU ARE ENOUGH

Most of us have the feeling that we are here to accomplish something big in our lives, and if we have not done anything that fits the bill, we may feel as if we are waiting. We may feel incomplete or empty, as if our lives do not yet make sense to us because they do not line up with our concept of a major accomplishment. In some cases, this may be because we really are meant to do something that we have not yet done. But in most cases, we can let ourselves off the hook with the realization that just being here, being ourselves, is enough.

As we live in this world, we share our energy and our spirit with the people around us in numerous ways. Our influence touches their lives and, through them, those of many more people. When we strive to live our lives to the fullest and to become our true selves, we are doing something big on an inner level, and that is more than enough for us to make sense of our being here on this planet at this time. There is no need to hold ourselves to an old idea in the back of our minds that we need to make headlines or single-handedly save the world in order to validate our existence.

We can each look within our hearts to discover what is true for us, what gives our lives meaning, and what excites us. We can release ourselves from any pressure to perform that comes from outside our inner sense of purpose. Staying in tune with our own values and living in tune with our own vision is all we need in order to fulfill our time here. Our lives are a process of *becoming,* so we cannot help but co-create; being who we are, responding to each moment as it comes, we can trust that this is enough.

INTEGRATING OUR MANY SELVES
THE SUM OF OUR PARTS

Human beings are multidimensional creatures. Our identity is made up of the sum of our many traits and values and our character. Each of us possesses within us many different selves. There is the adult part and the childlike spirit that resides within. There is our masculine side and our feminine side. There is the hard worker in us and the artist, the parent, and the caretaker. All of these selves combined form a well-rounded, complex person. Not all of these different aspects of who we are blend together easily, however, and some may even conflict with or oppose one another.

When our different parts clash—such as the self that is our childlike aspect and the self that is our responsible adult—we often end up compartmentalizing or suppressing one of these aspects to ease the conflict. While this may make us feel better in the short run, we would be better off finding a way for these two selves to coexist peacefully inside us.

Although some of our selves may be dominant, while others rarely assert themselves, attempts to suppress one or more of these different aspects can leave us feeling that our identity has been splintered. Being able to successfully integrate our various selves might be as simple as accepting and embracing each one. It may also be necessary to reframe the way we see them. The immature self that we ridicule can become a valued and accepted part of us when redefined as our more playful aspect. Journaling can help us acknowledge and understand the different parts that make up our identity.

When your many selves blend together to form an integrated individual, you will feel changed. You will no longer feel pulled in multiple directions, and you will never again have to deny any part of yourself. You become a complete person—familiar and comfortable with the many selves that make up who you are.

❧

WONDERFUL VESSEL
THE AMAZING BODY

As human beings, we have been given a wonderful gift. Our incredible minds and internal spirits are housed in bodies that enable us to physically connect with this beautiful planet we inhabit. We are able to see, hear, taste, smell, and feel through them and convey all those senses to our minds and souls so that we may learn and grow and ultimately evolve.

The human body serves us to the best of its ability every day of our lives, allowing us to breathe in the oxygen that is our life force, most of the time without our even having to think about it. That breath fuels a complex system that not only allows the body to function, but also to renew itself. Our bodies actually have the capacity to remake themselves at a cellular level every seven years. That we can heal from major injury, severe illness, and physical trauma is a feat that we often take for granted. When the mind and spirit are one with the body, our ability to heal ourselves is truly miraculous.

The conditions to which we humans are able to adapt are beyond what many other creatures on our planet can handle. Our bodies continually cleanse toxins, whether environmental or self-induced, from our system. We push them beyond their limits to perform incredible feats, jumping to heights unimaginable, running at speeds that break records, and bending into yoga postures that are beyond comprehension.

Even without sleep and nourishment, our bodies continue to function until there is no more to give. When one of our senses or organs ceases functioning, others are quick to step up to the plate and compensate for any loss. If we lose our eyesight, our hearing and/or other senses become more acute. When one kidney can no longer function, the other does the job for both of them. The human body is an incredible team that is on our side in the game of life.

We are blessed to be here, now, as human beings who can bring love and compassion to all the creatures we share this earth and universe with.

Honor your being and use it to do good. The spirit and mind are willing, and so, too, is the body.

❧⳾⳾☙

EMERGING COURAGEOUS
WALKING THROUGH YOUR FEAR

The situations, activities, and individuals that frighten us remain static. Their relative intensity does not change. Fear, on the other hand, self-magnifies. It is when we are afraid and envisioning all that might go wrong that the energy underlying our fear grows. A tiny flicker of anxiety can easily develop into terror that manifests itself physically and eventually paralyzes us into inaction. Frequently, though, in walking through that fear, we discover that its strength was out of sync with reality. And we learn that doing what frightens us can lead to great blessings. Confronting our trepidation head-on will help us accept that few frightening scenarios will ever live up to the disasters that we sometimes play out in our minds.

Although fear is an evolutionary gift meant to sharpen your senses and energize you during times of great stress, it can nonetheless become a barrier that prevents you from fulfilling your potential, by causing you to miss out on rewarding, life-changing experiences. During the period before you face your fear, you may have to deal with a barrage of negative thoughts and emotions. Walking through it—whether it is public speaking, taking part in an activity that makes you nervous, or asserting yourself when the odds are against you—may be equally difficult. But once you have emerged unscathed on the other side (which you will), you will probably wonder why you assumed the worst in the first place.

As you spend time worrying about what might happen, it is good to know that what you fear probably will not happen at all. It may feel like a great weight has been lifted from your shoulders, and you will likely feel a sense of passionate pride. Walking through your fear can mean taking risks and can require both practice and patience. Since it is challenging to act when you are gripped by fear, start small.

Each step you take into fear will strengthen you and help you confront future anxieties with poise, courage, and confidence. You will also find that when you are willing to stare your fear in the face, the universe will always offer you some form of aid or support. When you see the heights of accomplishment and personal evolution you can attain when you walk through your fears, your faith in yourself will grow, allowing your next step to be easier.

❦

PUTTING YOURSELF FIRST
MEETING YOUR OWN NEEDS

In life we are encouraged to think of others first. It is seen as a virtue to selflessly address the needs of parents, children, friends, and loved ones before—or sometimes at the cost of—our own. But this virtue, like any, is best and most meaningful in moderation. Overly caring for others can easily be an unconscious cry for love, or a crutch.

Devoting all of your time to others can stand in the way of your self-care. Taking care of yourself can feel selfish, while attending to those around you might seem easier than dealing with your own issues. But addressing *your* needs first in some cases is beneficial and vital not only to your own health and well-being, but to your ability to care for others when necessary.

We often find ourselves faced with too many responsibilities, and those most readily given up are often the most important to us. If this is true of you, ask yourself why. Do you feel the need to prove yourself by being selfless or hope your sacrifice will be acknowledged? Do you feel selfish for wanting things for yourself? Or is it simply more stressful to contemplate your own needs because they are the ones requiring the most personal effort on your part?

Selfless dedication can be frustrating when you do not find the appreciation or love you desire, which ironically leads you to put in more effort. But when you care for yourself, you affirm your own worth and boundaries. Do not be afraid to put yourself first now and then. Listen to your inner voice and be fair to yourself as well as to others. Have the courage to face *your* needs and issues head-on instead of putting them off by helping other people with theirs.

Not caring for yourself is often indicative of a great internal struggle. It can be helpful to recognize that you are as deserving of attention as any other human, and that you also function best when your needs are met. Try, when possible, to do something special for yourself, take a break, ask for help . . . and give your own needs the attention they deserve.

❧❦❧

LEARN AND LET FLOW
WE DO NOT NEED TO SUFFER

The idea that we have to suffer or live in poverty in order to be spiritual is an old one and can be found in the belief systems of many philosophies. Most of us carry this idea around subconsciously, and we may be holding ourselves back from financial or emotional well-being, believing that this is what we must do in order to act virtuously, be spiritually awake, or feel less guilty about the suffering of others.

While it is true that there can be a spiritual purpose to experiencing a lack of material well-being, it is rarely intended to be a permanent or lifelong experience. What we are meant to find when financial or emotional resources are in short supply is that there is more to our lives than the physical. Intense relationships and material abundance can distract us from the subtler realm of the spirit, so a time of deficiency can be spiritually awakening. However, once we recognize the realm of spirit and remember to hold it at the center of our lives, there is no reason to dwell in poverty or emotional isolation. In fact, once our connection to spirit is fully intact, we feel so compelled to share our abundance that lack becomes a thing of the past.

If you find that you are experiencing suffering in some area of your physical life, perhaps your spirit is asking you to look deeper in your search for what you want. For example, if you want money so that you can experience the feeling of security, but financial success keeps eluding you, your spirit may be asking you to understand that security is not to be found through money. Rather, it comes from an unshakable connection to your soul. Once you make that connection, prosperity will probably flow more easily into your life. If relationships elude you, your spirit may be calling you to recognize that the love you seek is not to be found in another person. And yet, ironically, once you find the love, your soul mate may very well appear. If you feel that you are stuck suffering in order to live a spiritual life, try to spend some time writing about it. The root of the problem will appear, and it may not be what you expected. Remember, the universe wants you to be happy.

❧✺❧

PART III
MAKING A CHANGE

There comes a time in the lives of most people when we realize that how we're living is just not working for us. Perhaps we've been unhappy for some time, been in an abusive relationship, or reached rock bottom with an addiction; or maybe we woke up one day and declared "Enough!"

I love change; everybody who knows me well understands this about me. I know that with change I'll face new challenges and hardships, my life will be turned upside down, and I'll probably be uncomfortable for a while.

My husband has learned to be accepting of this, and I usually try to warn him just before I hit the thick of it, and let him know how he can be supportive of me. Being in the midst of a life change can be messy, and if I'm not taking proper care of myself—body, mind, and spirit—I will spiral out of control, just like anybody else. It takes courage to face the challenge of life changes, and it also takes timing—you must be ready. Change is something that can't be forced; it needs to come from deep within, at a soul level, or you'll find yourself only going through the motions of change . . . and more than likely a part of you will rebel. If you're feeling like you want to make a change in your life—whether it involves your career, a relationship, a habit, or a move—there are steps you can take to help this process along:

1. Try to recognize where the feeling is coming from. Are you being told to change by somebody else, or are *you* really excited about it?

2. Next, journal about it and jot down what it is you want to change and why, and then write down what your expectations are after the change is complete. Journaling tells the universal energies that you are ready for this; you want this. The wheels will be set into motion, and you'll be brought circumstances to help facilitate your desire.

3. Think about the ways in which you normally sabotage your life and write those down so you can recognize the signs if and when they come up.

Sit with all this for a few days, allow your excitement to build, and begin taking baby steps toward your change—small things you can do to feel a sense of accomplishment. Allow the change to unfold naturally in your life without beating yourself up. This can happen quite fast; or depending on what it is you want to change, it may take a long time.

I don't necessarily love the process of change, because it is challenging, for sure, but I love when I come out on the other side of it. Not only did I survive, but I'm stronger and more empowered, I feel a sense of pride, and I know that no matter what happens, I don't ever have to go back to where I was.

But life can be like the proverbial onion, always another layer; or like a ladder, always another step. When you think you've addressed an issue and made the changes you want to, it's possible that you may be faced with a similar issue, but it will be at a deeper level. This is the onion. It isn't that you failed or took a step back; rather, it is your soul wanting to go deeper still. Your first reaction may be one of dismay that you worked so hard and here's this problem again! Fear not—you've done well, but your soul is signaling that you're ready to continue. This is the complete beauty of your soul: You won't get a nudge or a sign until you're ready, so in a way you can actually feel good about it. See it as an indication that you're strong rather than having the feeling of going back into the trenches.

Remember, too, that you always have free will; and if you're truly happy where you are now, then that's great. But if you have an inner knowing that keeps nudging you, saying that you'd like to make change, the universe will support you 100 percent. This I promise you, because I've seen it time and again in my own life.

One example of a change I wanted to make was to finally address my fear of crowds, public places, and public speaking. Unfortunately, I'd let this fear spiral out of control and found myself avoiding things I used to love, such as concerts and traveling—even going shopping. It kept popping up in my mind that it was time to address this, so I listened. I spent time journaling and meditating on why this was happening to me, when the behavior pattern started, and what it was that I was truly afraid of. I asked my guides and the universe for help. Slowly I was led to people who could help me, and each one held a unique piece of the puzzle.

Up until that time, it would have taken me an hour to leave the house while I put on all of my protective-gemstone jewelry, meditated to calm myself down, and brought in all of my angels and guides—it was sort of like trying to leave the house with ten screaming kids. But this alone wasn't enough for me . . . it took the edge off, but it wasn't getting to the root of the problem. So the universe sent me people with skills to help me.

From one wise woman I was given homework to do: when I was in a situation where I was feeling overwhelmed, I was to stop and tell my husband I was uncomfortable and hand him a list of questions to ask me. These questions helped ground me and make me realize I wasn't in danger.

I also received a lot of help from a past-life-regression therapist, who put me into a meditative state where I clearly saw myself as a barefoot maiden in a small European village. I was the village healer, and my power and medicinal practices with herbs scared people until one day they stoned me to death. No wonder I didn't like being in public! Usually I'm not one to rely on psychics or past-life regression for help because I'm now living in *this* lifetime, but it was very clear that this was an important aspect of my fear that had been carried over.

Because I was gifted with being a supersensitive in this life, I may not ever feel comfortable in crowds. I'm wired to be an empath (feeling the feelings of others) as part of my life path. But I can feel good about doing the hard work to address my fear, understand it better, and make change for the better.

One important part of change is trying to keep balance while you're in it—and afterward. I remember when I first learned to stop being a "yes" person, which comes from being a "good girl," and used my voice to say no. I was somewhat like a two-year-old: Everything was *no, no, no*. I was learning to invoke my power to disagree and have my own opinion, and not use the word *yes* so that people would like me. Soon I became a "no" person, but this needed to happen; it was a natural part of the cycle. Like with any change—or anything in life, really—it's all about balance.

When you're learning a new skill, you want to try it out—a lot. This is sure to cause an imbalance, but it's important to realize that it's also a part of the process: things will come out of balance before they settle into their new state of being. On a global scale, you can witness this by researching history—everything comes *out* of balance before it comes *into* balance. I believe this is one of the brilliant things about the universe. If you really think about it, doesn't it make sense? Everything is shown to us so we can learn; not only is it shown to us, but we need to actually *live* it so that our complete being fully understands the importance of balance. Eventually the pendulum will settle in the middle, that blissful place of balance and peace.

❦

Another aspect of change can be to put yourself in the driver's seat of your own life. How many people do you know who simply go through the motions of life and allow others to make their decisions for them? Maybe that describes *you:* somewhere along the way you gave up control of your own life. This process can happen slowly over the years, starting with controlling parents and then maybe marrying somebody who continues that pattern for you.

It isn't only our own families that take away our power of being in the driver's seat, but the media and government as well. We are told: "Eat this, but don't eat that," "This is good for you, but that isn't," and so on—repeatedly we receive messages to take away our own power. Nothing drives me crazier than to hear a person say, "But that's just the way it's done." Soon we all find that we're in the passenger seat, and some of us are even in the *backseat!* Being able to make a decision for ourselves is the ultimate in freedom.

The first step in making an informed decision is to research, and thank goodness for the Internet, which makes that so much easier. But even with research it's important to collect data from many sources, and only then can you make the best decision for yourself. When you've put yourself back in the driver's seat, you become somebody who participates in your own life and then out in the world. A new energy is born, an excitement; you're part of the game now and contributing not only to your own well-being, but to the energy of the whole.

✦

A phase of change that's often overlooked is saying goodbye to a part of ourselves that once was. This can come into physical form through the expression of feeling, like having the blues and even depression, as the old aspect of you that you're changing is being released. Another form it can take is a distinctive sense of fighting back, feeling like you're virtually digging your heels into the ground, kicking and screaming. The part of you that you're changing may have been with you for a long time, and maybe it isn't quite ready to go yet and is showing up in your life in some way.

Know that this is all normal and part of the cycle.

What I like to do is talk to it, write to it, or even have a ceremony, if needed, for that part of me that needs to go. You can think of it as a wake or a funeral for an aspect of yourself that is dying off. I then honor it and thank it for being with me and taking care of me, protecting me. Whatever its job was, I acknowledge it. I then let it know that it's time for it to go so that new light and change can come in.

This is something you've asked for and are ready for. For example, if you're coming to a place where you're ready to seek a relationship, there may be a part of you that's used to being alone and likes it, and another part that's scared of commitment or is feeling vulnerable. By talking to these parts of you and allowing them to fly free, you open the energy gate to receiving what you want.

STARTING SMALL
TAKING BABY STEPS IN LIFE

We all put off doing unpleasant chores, difficult tasks, or intimidating projects. The problem is that when we do so, we still have to tackle them sooner or later, and often procrastinating only makes things worse. It is helpful to start by taking baby steps toward doing anything that we feel stressed or fearful about.

Your first step might be to just write down what you want to accomplish—perhaps a list of housecleaning chores, paperwork, or things you have always wanted to do but felt apprehensive about, like taking scuba-diving lessons or reconnecting with estranged family members.

Another way of getting started is to give yourself a time limit. Again, start small and commit to 20 minutes of housework, for instance, or one hour of studying. You will probably find that once you start the task, it is not really that bad, and you will be able to give even more time to it. Then reward yourself with an afternoon at the beach or a movie.

Try to spend some time every day working on the tasks you want to complete. Finishing them will probably be reward enough, but you can always treat yourself to something special for a job well done.

You may have to take a different approach to things you feel apprehensive about, but again, baby steps can get you there. For instance, if you really want to learn to salsa dance but are afraid you might look foolish, start by renting a video so that you can practice at home. Your next step might be to try a class at a recreation center or community college rather than hitting a club. When you become familiar with the music and some basic steps, you will probably find that you enjoy dancing so much that you do not care what you look like. It is also good to remind yourself that everyone started at the beginning, even if they have been dancing for years.

In approaching people you feel intimidated by, you could start by composing a letter, even if you do not send it. Write down all the things you want to say, and rewrite the letter until you feel good about it. After that, you may want to send it, or you may feel ready to call the person or talk to him or her face-to-face.

Taking one step at a time can take you a long way toward your goals. If you trip or fall, just get back up and put one foot in front of the other. You will probably be there before you know it!

TEMPORARILY OUT OF BALANCE
GOING THROUGH A PHASE

We are all almost always in the process of learning something new, developing an underused ability or talent, or toning down an overused one. Some of us are involved in learning how to speak up for ourselves, while others are learning how to be more considerate. In the process of becoming, we are always developing and fine-tuning one or the other of our many qualities, and it is a natural part of this process that things tend to get out of balance. This may be upsetting to us or the people around us, but we can trust that it is a normal part of the work of self-development.

For example, we may go through a phase of needing to discover how to say no as a part of learning to set boundaries and take care of ourselves. During this time, we might say no to just about everything as a way of practicing and exploring this ability. Like a child who learns a new word, we want to try out this avenue of expression and empowerment as much as we can, because it is novel and exciting for us and we want to explore it fully. In this way, we are mastering a new skill, and eventually, as we integrate it into our overall identity, it will resume its position as one part of our balanced life.

In this process, we are overcompensating for a quality that was suppressed in our life, and the swinging of the pendulum from underuse to overuse serves to bring that quality into balance. Understanding what is happening is a useful tool that helps us be patient with the process. In the end, the pendulum settles comfortably in the center, restoring balance inside and out.

❦

LIFE TRANSITIONS
THE DEATH AND REBIRTH OF SELF

Sometimes a part of us must die before another can come to life. Even though this is a natural and necessary component of our growth, it is often painful, or if we do not realize what is happening, confusing and disorienting. In fact, confusion and disorientation are often the messengers that tell us a shift is taking place within us. These shifts happen throughout the lives of all humans as we move from infancy to childhood to adolescence and beyond. With each transition from one phase to another, we find ourselves saying goodbye to an old friend—the identity that we formed in order to move through that particular time.

Sometimes we form these identities in relationships or jobs, and when we shift, those areas of our lives become unsettled. Usually, if we take the time to look into the changing surface of things, we will find that a transformation is taking place within us. For example, we may go through one whole chapter of our lives creating a protective shell around ourselves because we need it in order to heal from some early trauma. One day, though, we may find ourselves feeling confined and restless, wanting to move outside the shelter we needed for so long; the new part of ourselves cannot be born within the confines of the shell that our old self needed to survive.

We may feel a strange mixture of exhilaration and sadness as we say goodbye to a part of ourselves that is dying and make way for a whole new identity to emerge in its place. We might find inspiration in working with the image of an animal that molts or sheds in order to make way for new skin, fur, or feathers to emerge. For example, keeping a duck feather or some other symbol of transformation can remind us that death and rebirth are simply nature's way of evolving. We can surrender to this process, letting go of our past self with great love and gratitude . . . and welcome the new with an open mind and heart, ready for the next phase of life.

❦

BACK IN THE DRIVER'S SEAT
THE PASSENGER

It is easy to go through this fast-paced world feeling as if we are being dragged through our weeks on the back of a wild horse. Many of us move from one thing to another until we end up back at home in the evening with just enough time to wind down and go to sleep, waking up the next morning to begin the wild ride once more. While this can be exhilarating for certain periods of time, a life lived entirely in this fashion can be exhausting; and more important, it places us in the passenger's seat when really we are the ones who should be driving.

When we get caught up in our packed schedules and our many obligations, weeks can go by without our doing one spontaneous thing or taking the time to look at the bigger picture of our lives. Without these breaks, we run the risk of going through our precious days on a runaway train. Taking time to view the bigger picture, asking ourselves if we are happy with the path we are on and making adjustments, puts us back in the driver's seat, where we belong. When we take responsibility for charting our own course in life, we may very well go in an entirely different direction from the one laid out for us by society and familial expectations. This can be uncomfortable in the short term, but in the long term it is much worse to imagine living this precious life without ever taking the wheel and navigating our own course.

Of course, time spent examining the big picture could lead us to see that we are happy with the road we are on, but we would like more time with family or more free time to do whatever we are drawn to at the moment. Even if we want more extreme changes, the way to begin is to get off the road for long enough to catch our breath and remember who we are and what we truly desire. Once we do that, we can take the wheel with confidence, driving the speed we want to go, in the direction that is right for us.

❦

TENDING THE EMOTIONS
HAVING A BREAKDOWN

Most of us have had the experience of holding back our emotions for so long that when they finally come out, we have something resembling a breakdown. For a certain period of time, the overwhelming flood of feelings coursing through our bodies consumes us, and we stop functioning. Often these outbursts take us by surprise, welling up within us as we drive to or from work, watch a movie, or engage in some otherwise mundane task. We may feel like we do not know what triggered us, or if we do know, it does not make sense of our overpowering emotional response. This is because we are releasing feelings that have accumulated over a long period of time, and whatever inspired the release was just a catalyst for a much larger catharsis.

When we find ourselves in the midst of such an experience, it is important that we allow it to happen, rather than fighting it or trying to shut it down. Wherever we are, we can attempt to find a private, safe place in which to let our feelings out. If we cannot access such a place immediately, we can promise to set aside some time for ourselves at our earliest possible convenience, perhaps taking a day off work. The important thing is that we need to give our emotional system some much-needed attention. It is essential that we allow ourselves to release the pent-up emotions inside us so that they do not create imbalances in our bodies and minds.

When you are feeling better, make a plan to find a way to process your emotions more regularly. You can do so by employing a therapist or making a regular date to talk to a trusted friend. Journaling can also be a great way to acknowledge and release your emotions, as can certain forms of meditation. Making room in your life for tending your emotions on a regular basis will keep you healthy, balanced, and ready for life.

❦

MARINATING
MAKING OUR BEST DECISIONS

Sometimes when we need to make a decision, we can become overwhelmed or feel pressured into coming to a conclusion immediately. Often a decision is not required right away, and the sense of urgency we feel is merely a limitation that we have placed upon ourselves. Once we have determined that we do have the time to make a wise choice for ourselves, we can release the pressure with a deep breath, like steam from a pressure cooker, and proceed to make the most beneficial use of our time.

The best first step may be to gather all the facts we can find. Once we have all the logical information we need, we can allow ourselves to sit with it and soak it up. Like a good recipe, we can let ourselves marinate in the juices of intellectual understanding while also adding our own spices made up of our feelings, our intuition, and any other considerations. We can taste the recipe for readiness as we go in order to decide if more time or ingredients are needed.

We might want to take a few moments to visualize ourselves playing out the various scenarios to see which feels best; remind ourselves of our goals; or merely sit silently in meditation, listening for guidance. Any of these techniques can add depth and flavor to the recipe of our decisions.

We can allow ourselves to sit with our choices for whatever length of time is needed, whether it is a day, a week, a month, or longer. Doing so gives our hearts, minds, and spirits the chance to align, allowing us to make a decision that is right for us. At other times we may need to let the wisdom of the universe unfold for us at its own rate, allowing our growth and realizations to synchronize with the universe's secret and essential ingredients so that all of the flavors are ready at the same time. When we allow ourselves the time to sit and allow understanding to sink in, we can co-create the best decision possible for ourselves and for everyone involved.

MIRACLES IN EVERY DAY
JOY ALWAYS

It is the everyday aspects of our lives that bring us the most joy, even if at first it may seem natural to expect our feelings of happiness to come from the larger events. By noticing how small things can fill our days with delight, we are more likely to experience the wonder of living. Once we take the time to look around and witness the beauty, kindness, and laughter that envelop us, what may seem like the ordinariness of the everyday becomes filled with the extraordinary detail of each individual moment. If we bring this sense of awareness to our lives for even a few minutes a day, we will begin to see just how blessed we truly are.

Beholding the joy that surrounds us may initially seem easy, but for some it can take a conscious effort to make it a part of a daily routine. When you awake in the morning and set the intention to notice more joy in the world, watch how your day and, eventually, your life is filled with it. The more you do so, the more apt you will be to notice the sounds of children laughing or the sparkle of dewdrops on a flower petal. Allow this joy to fill your heart fully, and from there it will naturally expand to your entire body and then spread to others, giving them joy as well.

Taking in the small joys of each day expands our feeling of being connected with the world, especially once we become more attuned to them. With every passing day, we will find that these small delights, which bring a deeper level of appreciation for everything the universe has given to our lives, are miracles.

BEING CLEAR ABOUT DESIRES
GETTING WHAT WE WANT

The best way to get what we want from life is to first *know* what we want. If we have not taken the time to really understand and identify what would truly make us happy, we won't be able to ask for it from those around us or from the universe. We may not even be able to recognize it when it arrives. Once we are clear about what we want, we can communicate it to those around us. When we can be honest about who we are and what we long for, there is no need to demand, be rude or aggressive, or manipulate others who are involved in helping us get what we want. Instead, we know that we are transmitting a signal on the right frequency to bring all that we desire into our experience.

As the world evolves, humanity is learning to work from the heart. We may have been taught that the way to get what we want is to follow certain rules, play particular games, or even engage in acts that use less than our highest integrity. The only rules we need to apply are those of intention and connection. In terms of energy, we can see that it takes a lot of effort to keep up a false front or act in a way that runs counter to our true nature, but much less is expended when we can just *be* and enjoy connections that energize us in return. Then our focus can be directed toward living the life we want right now.

Society has certain expectations of behavior and the roles each of us should play, but as spiritual beings, we are not bound by these superficial structures unless we choose to accept them. Instead, we can listen to our hearts and follow what we know to be true and meaningful for us. In doing so, we will find others who have chosen the same path. It can be easy to get caught up in following goals that appear to be what we want, but when we pursue the underlying value, we are certain to stay on our right path and continue to feed our souls.

THE EFFECT OF NOT DOING
WHEN WE DO NOT TAKE ACTION

Life is sculpted on a moment-to-moment basis. Every one of the thoughts we think, the words we speak, and the actions we take contributes to the complex quality and character of the universe's unfolding. It simply is not possible to be alive without making an impact on the world that surrounds us. Every action taken or not taken affects the whole. And when it comes to making the world a better place, what we choose *not* to do can be just as important as what we *do*.

For example, when we neglect to recycle, speak up, vote, or help somebody in immediate need, we are denying ourselves the opportunity to be agents for positive change. Instead, we are enabling a particular course to continue unchallenged, picking up speed even as it goes along. By holding the belief that our actions do not make much of a difference, we may find that we often tend to forgo opportunities for involvement. Alternatively, if we see ourselves as important participants in an ever-evolving world, we may feel more inspired to contribute our unique perspective and gifts to a situation.

It is wise to be somewhat selective about how and where we are using our energy in order to keep ourselves from becoming scattered. Not every cause or action is appropriate for every person. When a situation catches our attention, however, and speaks to our heart, it is important that we honor our impulse to help, and take the initiative that feels right for us. It may be offering a kind word to a friend, giving resources to people in need, or just taking responsibility for our own behavior. By doing what we can, when we can, we add positive energy to our world. And sometimes, it may be our one contribution that makes all the difference.

A GLIMPSE OF PERFECTION
LIVING A DAY IN GRACE

Grace is always with us. It flows like a river through our lives, artfully reminding us that there is magic and power beyond what our eyes can see. At times we catch its subtle beauty, like during chance meetings, near misses, and insights that seem to come from nowhere. At other times we experience grace in all its powerful surety, such as when a job or relationship comes to an end. Although we may forget that this is grace at work, too, it is indeed influencing our lives, helping us move forward and take the next step. Grace exists in all situations, in every moment, yet all too often we may overlook its presence.

Imagine how it would feel to live an entire day in grace, to fully appreciate that it is unfolding in absolute perfection. Whereas usually you might miss the magic in ordinary events and interactions, on this day you would recognize them all as little miracles. Perhaps you could begin with your first deep breaths in the morning, becoming aware that there is an abundant supply of air for you to breathe. Your lungs know just how to carry oxygen to your blood, which in turn knows where to carry it from there. This is grace at work. You might appreciate the brilliant sunshine, the warm summertime rain, or the possibilities for learning that greet you at every turn. You might notice the ease with which you do your job or laugh with a close friend. These things are also grace. Even laying your head down at the end of this day and resting in the stillness of night is grace.

With each opportunity you give yourself to enjoy this current of benevolence, you may discover a deeper sense of peace. Your faith may strengthen and your heart may open. You could begin to wonder if struggle is really all that necessary after all. By living this one day in grace, you might open the door to many more.

❦

ONE FOOT FORWARD
FINDING YOUR NEXT STEP IN LIFE

Our lives are made up of a complex network of pathways that we can use to move from one phase of life to the next. For some of us, our paths are wide, smooth, and clearly marked. Many people, however, find that they have a difficult time figuring out where they need to go next. Determining which "next step" will land us along the most direct route to fulfillment and the realization of our life purpose may not seem easy.

There are many ways to discover what the next step on your life path should be. If you are someone who seeks to satisfy your soul, it is vital that you make this inquiry. Often your inner voice will counsel you that it is time for a change, and it is very important to trust yourself, because only you know what is best for you. Personal growth always results when you let yourself expand beyond the farthest borders of what your life has been so far. When figuring out what your next step will be, you may want to review your life experiences. The choices you have made and the dreams you have held on to can give you an idea of what you do not want to do anymore and what you might like to do next.

It is also a good idea to think about creative ways you can use your skills and satisfy your passions. Visualizing your perfect future and making a list of ways to manifest that future can help you choose a logical next step that is in harmony with your desires. Meditation, journal writing, taking a class, and other creative activities may inspire you and provide insight regarding the next step in life that will bring you the most satisfaction.

It is when you are willing to listen to yourself and be fearless that figuring out your next step becomes easy. Beneath the fear and hesitation and uncertainty lies your inner knowing that always perceives which one needs to come next. If you can allow the taking of your next step to be as easy as putting one foot in front of the next, you will notice that it is always . . . right in front of you. All you have to do is put one foot forward.

⊷❦⊶

SIGNING ON THE DOTTED LINE
MAKING A CONTRACT WITH YOURSELF

Our decisions in life—what we change about ourselves and how we choose to react—are no one's responsibility but our own. But because the mind often rebels against what we know in our souls to be positive changes, putting a plan of improvement in action can be difficult.

One very useful tool to help bring about change is to make a contract with yourself. A self-contract, like any other, is a formal written commitment and can be drafted for an infinite number of reasons. It is an agreement between you and yourself that can act as a guide, motivator, means to enact self-improvement, or way of making peace with yourself. You choose an aspect of your life you would like to focus on and then lay out in clear language what you want to do, how you will do it, and if you wish, a timetable.

Be honest and make sure what you include reflects attainable goals. A contract that you cannot bring yourself to follow is not going to be very helpful. In writing it, specify why you have created it, your responsibilities and the results you expect, what reward you will give yourself (if appropriate), and the individual steps you will take. Date and sign it, alone or in the presence of a witness. If it helps, you can make a ceremony out of the signing.

Motivations for entering into a contract with yourself may include changing a behavior or working through a personal issue. Reading the contract daily can help you remain committed to the guidelines you have laid out for yourself. Abiding by them shows that you take your commitment seriously and will treat yourself with the honesty and respect you deserve.

❧❦❧

PART IV

SEEKING KNOWLEDGE AND WISDOM

When we begin our paths to awareness, it's very common to be like sponges and want to learn everything possible; our curiosity is piqued, and we hunger to know more. We may devour books, attend classes and workshops, and do research online to try to satiate our craving for information. The hungry mind is an exciting mind.

I've always been a person who seeks knowledge from many different sources: I take it all in and then use what feels right to me, and I discard the rest. Some people feel comfortable following a guru or being a devotee of a particular practice. It doesn't really matter which path you take as long as it feels completely right in your heart and you aren't receiving any red flags from your intuition that something may *not* be right.

There are many different paths, and each one appeals to different people based on their own life experiences or upbringing. There is no "right" way, and it's very possible that *your* way may be completely different from those of the individuals in your inner circle.

❧

At one particular point in my life, it seemed like I was around a bunch a complainers—everywhere I went, everything I read or watched, somebody was complaining. When I went into meditation about this, I received strong guidance to let people know that it is important to be *for* something rather than the opposite. People who have realized this and are *for* something seem to have gotten to the place where they understand the wisdom in this concept. People are "anti" this and that, and I could see and feel how much energy was being wasted in the negativity. I kept thinking that if they could harness all of that negative energy and focus it in the other direction, their mission would be so much easier! Energy flows so much more readily in the presence of positivity and hopefulness.

I started to apply this in my own life on smaller, everyday issues and immediately noticed an improvement in my outlook. Minor things like traffic, bills, and rude people started not to bother me as much. It was like I jumped onto a positive-energy wave and rode it all day.

Take a moment to think about what things in your life you're against, and see if you can turn the energy into a positive force rather than a negative one.

❧

As human beings, we learn and absorb information differently; what works for one person may not work for another. Thank goodness we are all different . . . can you imagine living in a world where everybody was the same? Not very exciting, and probably downright boring.

I'm a very visual and experiential person: I need a story, maybe a graph or drawing, and then some good old life experience to back it all up. I can't learn from a lecture. I don't retain information from just being talked to, but some people do learn in this way, more so than they do visually. For a long time I thought I was stupid because I didn't learn in the way I was supposed to—school was a nightmare for me because I wasn't being taught in the style that I needed. "One size fits all" doesn't seem to work very well for a school system.

The same thing applies to one's awakening and journey in life. One person may require a guru or feel the need to travel to a sacred place, whereas another may only need to sit in the living room and meditate every day. Some people find their spiritual selves by attending church or applying religion to their lives, while others may be appalled by those ideas and seek a path on their own. One way isn't better than the other—what matters is getting to that place of peace within yourself.

❦

GATHERING INTELLIGENCE
DIFFERENT WAYS OF KNOWING

We human beings have many ways of knowing what we need to in order to get through our lives. One way of doing so is to engage in a course of study in an academic environment. Another is simply to go through the experiences that come our way, making a conscious effort to learn from them. A third way in which people gain knowledge is through the vehicle of intuition, a gift some possess more than others, but which can be developed in anyone. No one way of knowing things is better than another, and they can all be useful at different points in our lives.

Most of us naturally gravitate toward one way of knowing over others, and this tends to be clear early on. For the most part, we live in a culture that values a logical, mental approach to things, so those with intuitive gifts may have been shamed, undervalued, or misunderstood. Many of us are working our way out of this incorrect value judgment, recognizing that our intuition, far from being wrong or untrustworthy, is a great gift. For those of us who conduct our learning in the thick of our life experiences, we may also have to make an extra effort to remind ourselves that our particular intelligence—often called common sense—while not always officially rewarded, has its own special genius.

Even though in a given time or place certain types of intelligence tend to be valued more than others, no way of knowing is inherently better than another. Once we understand this, we can value our own intelligence, as well as the different levels and types of intellect in the people we encounter. Sometimes just understanding that we are coming at the same issue in different ways helps us avoid unnecessary conflict. When we value all ways of knowing equally, we benefit not only from what we have learned and how we have learned it, but from all the other forms of intelligence we are open to honoring.

❦

OWNING YOUR TENDENCIES
UNDERSTANDING ALL SIDES

Whenever we examine our lives, we do so from a particular side or angle. Most of us tend to favor a single side over the others. For example, we may tend to look at things from an emotional perspective rather than a financial one, or we may prefer to think in terms of details rather than the big picture—or vice versa. To a certain degree, this is not a problem, and these tendencies add color to our individual personalities. However, they can also make us one-sided, blind to the many other ways of looking at our situation. Even if we have decided that we are most happy when we focus on a particular side of things, it is always worth exploring the others. When we do, we become well-rounded, more understanding of other viewpoints, and even more solid in our own.

Perhaps you are a person who tends to see your life in terms of your spiritual well-being. As a result, other concerns, such as financial comfort or social standing, may not be prominent in your mind as you make decisions. However, taking just a moment to consider those angles will help you in several ways: (1) it will enable you to see more clearly what your priorities are and how they influence your life situation; (2) it will enhance your sense of confidence, because you will see your situation from all sides, even as you choose one; and (3) it will help you communicate with others about who you are and what you are doing, because you will understand that your own biases and tendencies are unique, as are theirs.

Most of us instinctively come at things from a particular angle, and in many cases this is the right way for us. Still, understanding the other angles only strengthens us. When we look at our lives from all sides, we shed light on the big picture, giving ourselves access to many points of view and highlighting more clearly the one we have chosen.

❦

SPIRITUAL DIVERSIFICATION
EXPANDING YOUR SOURCES OF GROWTH

There are numerous fountains of spiritual knowledge, although many choose to drink from only one. While delving deeply into a single discipline can lead to a strong core of knowledge, there are innumerable benefits to gleaning information from many sources. Truth can be found in anything, and spirituality is a thing of many dimensions. Personal growth should involve individual awareness, testing theories, and learning through others. As a result, much can be learned by experiencing a wide variety of faiths, rituals, practices, and individuals. In this way, you may find aspects of various sources of knowledge that appeal to you, empowering you to customize your method of spiritual growth.

Nothing is lost when you embrace multiple paths, and much is gained. You can explore without having to immediately adhere to rigid guidelines and limit yourself to one practice. You also open your soul to finding inspiration from a great cache of locations, individuals, texts, and methods. That openness can help you both achieve an elevated sense of awareness that eclipses narrow-mindedness and be more content with and accepting of the unexpected. Maintaining a dialogue with multiple teachers can lead to fresh approaches and vitality in your spiritual growth, because you will always have access to multiple solutions to any problem. Learning from a variety of sources involves listening to others without prejudice, welcoming new ideas, and seeking out guidance in novel places. You may also want to experiment on your own to develop personalized spiritual techniques in terms of meditation and other practices.

There are many orientations and many belief systems in the world, each offering numerous viewpoints and paths to enlightenment. There are thousands of teachers and texts from which to learn. Use your ears and your eyes, but also use your heart in choosing the sources from which you draw knowledge. Never forget that you are entitled to take the time to find your own unique path, and in fact it can be very empowering.

❦❦❦❦

PUTTING POWER
IN PERSPECTIVE
ALWAYS BE *FOR* SOMETHING

As human beings, we cannot help but be subject to our preferences. However, we do have control over the manner in which these manifest themselves in our lives. Every value we hold dear is an expression either of support or opposition, and it is our perspective that determines whether we are *for* something or *against* it.

As an example of a situation we are all familiar with: We can direct our energy and intention into activities that promote peace rather than using our resources to speak out in opposition of war. On the surface, these appear to be two interchangeable methods of expressing one virtue, yet being *for* something is a vastly more potent means of inspiring change because it carries with it the power of constructive intent.

When you support a cause, whether your support is active or passive, you contribute to the optimism that fuels all affirmative change. Optimistic thoughts energize people, giving them hope and inspiring them to work diligently on behalf of what they believe in. Being *for* something creates a positive shift in the universe, which means that neither you nor those who share your vision will have any trouble believing that transformation on a grand scale is indeed possible. To be *against* something is typically easy, as you need only speak out in opposition to it. Standing up *for* something is often more challenging, because you may be introducing an idea to people that may scare them on a soul level.

Throughout your life, you have likely been told that the actions of one person will seldom have a measurable impact on the world. Yet your willingness to stand up for what you believe in, instead of decrying what you oppose, can turn the tides of fate. The thoughts you project when you choose to adopt a positive perspective will provide you with a means to actively promote your values and, eventually, foster lasting change.

THE ULTIMATE AUTHORITY
USING OUR OWN MINDS

To a certain degree, we rely on other people's accounts of reality to inform us of the nature of the universe. For example, we cannot all be molecular physicists, but we can benefit from taking scientific findings to heart. In the same way, we often look to teachers, various leaders, and gurus to tell us about the path to enlightenment and the nature of the realm of spirit. While this input from experts is undeniably valuable, our own sense of the truth is ultimately the most important piece in processing the information we take in from external sources. In the end, we are the authorities in our own lives, and we have the final say on whether something generally held as true is true for *us*.

We need only take a brief look at history to remember that the religious, scientific, and political establishments that ruled the day were all wrong about something at some point in time. This is the beauty of learning, experiencing, and evolving. While we sometimes wish we could just let someone else decide for us what is real and true, this is clearly not a viable option. The good news in all this is that we can confidently devote ourselves to making up our own minds about reality, taking everything that is handed to us as truth with a grain of salt.

This does not mean that we discount the information we receive from outside sources. It simply means that we are vigilant enough to question it before we decide whether or not we agree with it. All the input we receive is useful in the process of helping us make up our own minds. As we allow ourselves to sit with the things we learn, measuring them alongside our own inner sense of the truth and our own experiences, we find that making up our minds is a joyful process of integration that grows us into stronger, smarter, more engaged human beings.

❦

EMBRACING
NEW INFORMATION
BE OPEN

Living in an information age, it is easy to become overwhelmed by the constant influx of scientific studies, breaking news, and even spiritual revelations that fill our bookshelves, radio waves, and in-boxes. No sooner have we decided what to eat or how to think about the universe than a new study or book comes out confounding our well-researched opinion. After a while, we may be tempted to dismiss or ignore new information in the interest of stabilizing our point of view—and this is understandable. Rather than closing down, we might try instead to remain open by allowing our intuition to guide us.

For example, contradictory studies concerning which foods are good for you and which ones are bad for you are plentiful. At a certain point, though, we can decide for ourselves whether coffee or tomatoes are good for us or not. The answer is different for each individual, and this is something that a scientific study cannot quite account for. All we can do is take in the information and process it through our own systems of understanding. In the end, only we can decide which concepts we will integrate. Remaining open allows us to continually change and shift by checking in with ourselves as we learn new information. It keeps us flexible and alert, and while it can feel a bit like being thrown off balance all the time, this openness is essential to the process of growth and expansion.

Perhaps the key is realizing that we are not going to finally get to some stable place of having it all figured out. Throughout our lives, we will go through the processes of opening up to new information, integrating it, and stabilizing our worldview. No sooner will we have reached some kind of stability than it will be time to open up again to new information, which is inherently *de*stabilizing. If we see ourselves as surfers riding the incoming tides of information and inspiration, always willing to attune ourselves to the next shift, we will see how blessed we are to have this opportunity to play on the waves and, most of all, to enjoy the ride.

❦

GATHERING OUR STRAYING THOUGHTS
CENTERING OURSELVES

When our thoughts are scattered in several directions at once and we are no longer conscious of what we are doing or why, it is time to center ourselves. To do so, we begin by acknowledging that we have become spread too thin and are no longer unified inside. Our thoughts might be out of sync with our feelings, and our actions may be out of sync with both. The main signs that we need to center ourselves are scattered thoughts and a feeling of disconnection or numbness, as if we are no longer able to take anything in. In addition, we may feel unfocused and not present in our bodies. Centering ourselves is a way of coming to terms with all the different energies within us and drawing them back into ourselves.

Centering yourself means that you are working from, or being aware of, the core of your being in the solar-plexus area of your body. At first it may not make sense, but as you progress, you will understand what this feels like.

We naturally know how to center ourselves when, for example, we take a deep breath before making a big announcement or doing something important. Another way to go about it is to sit down and engage in breath meditation. We can start by simply getting into a comfortable upright position and noticing as our breath enters and leaves our bodies. Our breath flows into and out from our center, and this process can serve as a template for all of our interactions in the world. In conversations, we can take what our friends are saying into the center of our beings and respond from there. Our whole lives mirror this ebb and flow of energy that begins and ends at the center of ourselves. If we follow this ebb and flow, we are in harmony with the universe, and when we find we are *out* of harmony, we can always come back into balance by sitting down and observing our breath.

When we sit down to center ourselves, we can imagine that we are gathering our straying thoughts and energies back into us, the way a mother duck gathers her babies around her. We can also visualize casting a net and pulling all the disparate parts of ourselves back to the center of our being, creating a sense of fluid integration. From this place of centeredness, we can begin again, directing ourselves outward in a more intentional way.

⬧⬥⬦⬥⬧

UNEARTHING YOUR ROOTS
KNOWING YOUR HISTORY

Each of us is a piece of a larger puzzle. We are all born into the unique and complex network of individuals, settings, and circumstances that constitute our heritage.

Whether or not you are aware of your ancestors, your family's country of origin, the cultural history of your people, or the trials faced by those responsible for bringing you into the world, these forces have had a hand in shaping your values. Knowing your family history and reflecting often upon your own personal history as it relates to your heritage empowers you to look at your life in a larger context and to understand that you are a vital part of an ongoing drama greater than yourself.

Researching your heritage can prepare you to meet the future. The traits of your ancestors give you insight into how your character has developed and the beliefs that form the foundation of your worldview. The knowledge you gain could help you appreciate your values and your character, giving you the confidence to be more expressive where both are concerned. At a cellular level, you carry a genetic code from your family, determining things like how you age, your blood type, and personality traits. But as a spiritual being, you bring in what you choose to do with that genetic coding—your free will. Unearthing your heritage is not simply about uncovering who did what when or reconnecting with long-lost relatives. Rather, it is a method of building self-awareness and bridging the gulf that divides your past from your future.

In researching our individual histories, however, we may encounter relatives who made interesting choices or were involved in traumatic events. It is easy to overestimate the importance of these pieces of our pasts and to cling to them. Balance is key.

While your heritage has influenced the development of the person you are today, you are more than an ethnicity, a culture, or a family name. You should not feel driven to alter your likes, dislikes, dreams, preferences, or values because you feel your heritage demands it. Knowing your history is about loving who you are, understanding where you have come from, and preparing for your future.

❦

BREAKING THE WAVE
THE TIPPING POINT

Those who desire change are often counseled to expect small transformations and rewards that reveal themselves slowly. And the most profound adjustments in how people perceive the world often do occur gradually, with clear relationships between cause and effect. But ideas can be contagious, spreading little by little from one individual to another, with no noticeable societal change . . . no large-scale change, that is, until a critical mass has been reached. At that point—the *tipping point*—the idea is accelerated and rushes forward, almost unstoppable. It can be something concrete, such as the widespread interest in a fad; or something more cerebral, such as growing spiritually, enlightenment, or experiencing an awakening of consciousness.

To visualize the tipping point, think of a wave composed of individual drops of water representing people. As people embrace a movement or method—be it Buddhism, yoga, a goddess, or meditation—they increase the wave.

As greater numbers benefit from it, the wave grows, until it reaches its peak and plunges forward, actively drawing people in without their being aware of any change at all. At that point, the idea, social behavior, or trend begins to spread at an amazing rate.

When applied to the context of an awakening consciousness, one person may assist another, who in turn may help another. But the spread will only progress from individual to individual until the tipping point is reached. When the critical mass is achieved, it becomes almost futile to resist that awakening, and the whole of a group or even the whole of humanity may be transformed.

The tipping point is a period of change wherein a creative minority can make a tangible difference by spreading positive ideas to the majority. It only takes a single individual to "tip" the wave. In applying the concept of the tipping point to your own growth, it may be helpful to remember the power of one. It means no effort is useless, because it is contributing to a larger outcome, and even small actions can produce profound changes.

❦

NOT ALONE IN THE DARK
LOOKING AT WHAT WE DO
NOT WANT TO SEE

It is one of life's great paradoxes that the things we do not want to look at in ourselves are the very things we *need* to look at in order to know ourselves better and to become more fully who we are. The feelings that make us want to run away are buried treasures full of energy and inspiration if we are willing to examine them. These feelings assume many forms, from strange images or snippets of information to recurring dreams and sensations that rise up seemingly without a reason. Whatever shape they come in, and no matter how scary they seem, these messengers bring the information we need in order to grow.

When we are tired of pushing something away or trying to run from it, a good first step is to write down what we think we are avoiding. Often this turns out to be only the surface of the issue or a symbol of something else. Expressing ourselves fully on paper is a safe way to begin exploring the murky territory of the unconscious. The coolness of the intellect can give us the distance we need to read what we have written and feel less afraid of it. It helps if we remember that no matter how dark or negative our thoughts or feelings may be, these are energies shared by all of humanity. We are not alone in the dark, and all the gurus and teachers we admire had to go through their own unprocessed emotional territory in order to come out the other side brighter and wiser.

Within the parts of ourselves that we do not want to look at, there are emotions that need to be felt. Unfelt emotions are forms of stuck energy, and when we leave them unprocessed, we deprive ourselves of access to that energy. When we feel strong enough, we can begin the process of experiencing those emotions, on our own or with guidance from a spiritual counselor. It is through this work that the buried treasure of energy and inspiration will pour forth from our hearts, giving us the courage to look at all the parts of ourselves with insight and compassion.

❦

THE PAST IN
LIGHT OF THE PRESENT
KNOWING BETTER NOW

When we look back on the past knowing what we know now, we often find it difficult to understand how we made the mistakes we made. This is because once we acquire new information, it is nearly impossible to reenter the head space we were in before. And so we look back at parents who spanked their kids, for example, and wonder how they could have thought that was a good idea. Similarly, our personal pasts are full of mistakes we cannot believe we made. We did things then that we would never do now, and this is precisely because we have information now that we did not have, or were not able to access, then.

From ideas about how to raise children to how to treat the environment, our collective human past sometimes reads like a document on what *not* to do. In many ways, this is exactly as it should be. We learn from living and having experiences. It is from these past actions that we garnered the information that guides us to live differently now. In our personal lives, we probably had to go through a few unsuccessful relationships or jobs, and thereby learn about our own negative tendencies, in order to gain the wisdom we currently possess.

In order to live more peacefully with the past, it helps to remember that once we know better, we tend to *do* better. Prior to knowing, we generally try our best, and while it is true that from the perspective of the present, our best does not always seem good enough, we can at least give our past selves the benefit of the doubt. We did what we could with the knowledge we had. Beyond this, we serve the greater good most effectively by not dwelling on the past; instead, reining our energy and knowledge into our present actions. It is here, in this moment, that we create our reality and ourselves anew, with our current knowledge and information.

❧⁂☙

PART V

THE IMPORTANCE
OF FAMILY AND FRIENDS

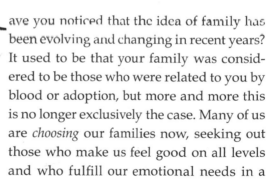

ave you noticed that the idea of family has been evolving and changing in recent years? It used to be that your family was considered to be those who were related to you by blood or adoption, but more and more this is no longer exclusively the case. Many of us are *choosing* our families now, seeking out those who make us feel good on all levels and who fulfill our emotional needs in a healthy, nonjudgmental way. Some do so because they have no blood relatives left or live a long way from them; others because they aren't vibrating at the same energy level as their birth family.

I wouldn't be surprised if you've always felt like the "black sheep" in *your* family . . . that is, you feel that nobody understands you, or how you live your life. This is common when you're a person stepping into awareness and full consciousness; you may have felt this way since you were a child, or it can happen later in life as you start your journey to self-fulfillment. It's important, though, to always remember your blood family even if you don't feel you have any connection with them.

The best thing you can do is always be yourself . . . there's no need to reinvent yourself when you're around your family or downplay your light or your way of life. By being yourself, you're sharing the gift of your energy, which—believe it or not—is being recognized by your family members on a subtle level. It may not be their path in this lifetime to share the interests that you have, and it isn't your job to try to convert anybody to the way you live.

I've always felt like a big misfit in my extended family. Nobody else meditates or has any metaphysical interests whatsoever, and I've asked many times, *What am I doing in this family?* Over the years, they've learned to accept me and I them. I can't ask for any more, and I feel satisfied and content with our relationship.

❧

I enjoy watching young children: they lovingly and without judgment accept all other children into their world. For adults it is much harder to make friends, as we come to the table with all of our angst, trauma, and learned behaviors. Most of my life I've been a loner—I really enjoy being in quiet solitude with my thoughts. But somewhere along the line as my life began to be healed, I realized that I had also become lonely; I hadn't taken the time to cultivate and maintain any close friendships.

Starting over in my mid-30s and trying to make friends seemed like an impossible task . . . I couldn't wrap my head around the idea that somebody might actually want to be

friends with me, consi
and hang-ups. But it w
I created amazing frie
for who I am, just as I a
had to learn from scr
as it was so foreign to
and some close ones
wasn't behaving as a

All of this taugh
learn new skills abo
like a daunting ta
become very easy
of meeting new pe

I've found tha
tain purpose or
away and lose t
simply don't see
one of us has ch
know that it's o
and even some

Everybody
mix, and som
relationship
the judgmen
friendship fo
from it.

THE POWER BEHIND US
PEOPLE WHO SUPPORT US

Behind each of us stands at least one supporter. This was once thought to be the spouse who ran the home, leaving the remaining spouse free to work. While this is still a valid scenario, most of us will find that we have other kinds of supporters in our lives. In some cases, these are the people whose help allows us to do the things we are best at, see to our obligations, or pursue our dreams. In other cases, our support may come from the people who are there to help us through life's challenges by offering us their strength and bolstering our spirits.

Our support may come from our families and friends or from the people we hire—nannies, assistants, gardeners, healers, therapists, and advisors. Our supporters may be the mentors who help us express ourselves by listening to us as we share our thoughts and feelings. They can include the person sitting next to us at a networking meeting or the teacher from our childhood whose words still resonate in our minds. We have always had supporters around us, whether we noticed them or not. No matter where the assistance comes from, few of us can make it through life unaided.

As we take the time to acknowledge everyone who has ever supported us, we cannot help but feel grateful. Understanding our place in our human support system lets us see that just as there are people who support us, *we* are supporters to many people. By gratefully accepting the expertise and assistance of our supporters, we can consciously and more easily build a life we love.

Give thanks to staff, friends, and loved ones for all their support. We all need each other's help to thrive in this world.

DISAPPROVING FACES
NOT EVERYBODY WILL LIKE YOU

It is not necessarily a pleasant experience, but there will be times in our lives when we come across people who do not like us. As we know, like attracts like, so usually when these individuals do not like us, it is because they are not *like* us. Rather than taking it personally, we can let them be who they are, accepting that each of us is allowed to have different perspectives and opinions. When we give others that freedom, we claim it for ourselves as well, releasing ourselves from the need for their approval so we can devote our energy toward more rewarding pursuits.

While approval from others is a nice feeling, when we come to depend on it, we may lose our way on our own path. There are those who will not like us no matter what we do, but that does not mean that there is anything wrong with us. We each have our own filters built from our experiences over time. Others may see in us something that is merely a projection of *their* mind-set, but we have no control over such interpretations. The best we can do is to hope that the role we play in the script of their lives is helpful to them, and then follow our own inner guidance with integrity.

As we reap the benefits of walking our perfect paths, we grow to appreciate the feeling of fully being ourselves. The need to have everyone like us will be replaced by the exhilaration of discovering that we are attracting like-minded individuals into our lives—people who like us because they understand and appreciate the truth of who we are. We free ourselves from trying to twist into shapes that will fit the spaces provided by others' limited under-standing and gain a new sense of freedom, which allows us to expand into becoming exactly who we are meant to be. And in doing what we know to be right for us, we show others that they can do it, too. Co-creating our lives with the universe and its energy of pure potential, we transcend limitations and empower ourselves to shine our unique light, fully and freely.

❦❖❦

THE DANCE OF INTIMACY
COMING BACK TO
CENTER IN A RELATIONSHIP

Anyone in a long-term relationship knows that the dance of intimacy involves coming together and moving apart. Early on, intense periods of closeness are important in order to establish the ground of a new union. Just as a sapling needs a lot more attention than a full-grown tree does, budding relationships demand time and attention if they are to fully take root. Once the union becomes more established, the individuals begin to turn their attention outward again, to the other parts of their lives that matter, such as work, family, and friendships. This is natural and healthy. Yet, if a long-term relationship is to last, turning toward one another regularly—with the same curiosity, attention, and nurturance of earlier times—is essential.

In a busy and demanding world full of obligations and opportunities, we sometimes lose track of our primary relationships, thinking they will tend to themselves.

We may have the best intentions when we consider how nice it would be to surprise our partner with a gift or establish a weekly date night. Yet somehow life gets in the way. We may think that our love is strong enough to survive without attention. Yet even mature trees need water and care if they are to thrive.

One of the best ways to nourish a relationship is through communication. If you feel that a distance has grown between you and your partner, you may be able to bridge the gap by sharing how you feel. Do your best to avoid blame and regret. Focus instead on the positive: the fact that you want to grow closer. Sometimes just acknowledging that there is distance between you has the effect of bringing the relationship into balance. In other cases, more intense effort and attention may be required. You might want to set aside time to talk and come up with solutions together. Remember to have compassion for each other. You are both in the same boat, trying to maintain the right balance of space and together-ness to keep your relationship healthy and thriving. Express faith and confidence in each other, and enjoy the slow dance of intimacy that can resume between the two of you.

❦

SHARING GRIEF
OPENING UP TO RECEIVE COMFORT

When we experience something that causes us shock and sadness, we may feel the urge to withdraw from life. It might seem like remaining withdrawn will keep us protected from the world, but during these times it is important to reach out to those trusted and precious people who care about us most. Even with our best knowledge and reasoning, we never know when someone else's experience or perspective can give us additional information that we need. The universe speaks to us through many channels, and when we open ourselves up to receive its messages, we also receive nurturing care from a loving partner in life's journey.

Grief is part of the human experience, and sharing our vulnerability is what creates truly close bonds in our relationships. Opening ourselves up in this way gets to the core of our being, past all of our defenses and prejudices. When life seems to crack the outer shell of our world, we are simultaneously raw and fresh. It is then that we discover who is truly willing to walk through life with us. We also see that some of those sent to us may not be the ones we expected to see. Regardless, we learn to trust in the universe, in others, in our own strength and resilience, and in the wisdom of life itself.

Sharing grief allows us to ease our burdens by letting someone else help carry them. This helps us process our own inner thoughts and feelings through the filter of trusted and beloved advisors. We may feel guilty or selfish, as if we are unloading on those who have their own challenges . . . although, if we think about it, we know we would do the same for them, and their protests would seem pointless. Remember that not sharing feelings with others denies them the opportunity to feel. We may be the messengers sent by the universe for their benefit, and it is on this mission that we have been dispatched. By sharing our hopes, fears, joys, and pains with another person, we accept the universe's gifts of wisdom and loving care.

LITTLE GURUS
LEARNING TO FOLLOW

As grown-ups, we often approach children with ideas about what we can teach them about life—something to which they are so recently arrived. It is true that we have important information to convey, but children are here to teach *us* just as much as we are here to teach *them*. They are new to the world and far less burdened with preconceived notions about the people, situations, and objects they encounter. They do not avoid others on the basis of appearance, nor, for example, do they regard shoes as having only one function. They can be fascinated for half an hour with a pot and a lid, and they are utterly unselfconscious in their emotional expressions. They live their lives fully immersed in the present moment, seeing everything with the open-mindedness born of unknowing. This enables them to inhabit a state of spontaneity, curiosity, and pure excitement about the world that we, as adults, have a hard time accessing. Yet almost every spiritual path calls upon us to rediscover this way of seeing. In this sense, children are truly our gurus.

When we approach children with the awareness that they are our teachers, we automatically become more present ourselves, as we have to be more so when we follow, looking and listening, and responding to their lead. We do not lapse so easily into the role of the director of activities, surrendering instead to having no agenda at all. As we allow our children to determine the flow of play, they pull us deeper into the mystery of the present moment. In this magical place, we become innocent again, unsure of what will happen next and remembering how to let go.

Since we must also embody the role of loving guide to our children, they teach us how to transition gracefully from following to leading and back again. In doing so, we learn to dance with our children in the present moment, shifting and adjusting as we direct the flow from pretending to be kittens wearing shoes on our heads to making sure everyone is fed and bathed.

❧⸙☙

FREEING OUR INNER DESIRES
USING OUR "OUTSIDE" VOICES

Each of us has developed an internal filtering process that helps us choose which parts of our constant inner monologues get voiced outside of our heads. Sometimes the choice is based on what we consider to be polite or appropriate, using subtlety instead of directness to try to get our point across. Other times it is based on our expectations of the other person and what we feel he or she should know about us, our feelings, and our needs. But our best chance of getting what we need is to communicate specifically by converting our inner voices to our outside ones.

This may seem unnecessary sometimes, especially when we think others have the same information we ourselves are working with, but we have to remember they also have their own inner voices, evaluating what they hear in light of *their* issues and needs. With so much to consider and sift through, we are truly better off if we communicate precisely. Not only does doing so minimize the chances of misinterpretation, but voicing our thoughts is an act of creation. We convert idea and imagination to sound, releasing it from the chamber of our minds into the outside world. This carries energy and intention with it, making our thoughts, wishes, and even our dreams come true.

When we have the courage to speak our minds and use our voices to send our hearts' desires from our inner world to the one outside, we take a bold step in manifesting them. By removing the fear of what others may think, as well as the expectations of what they should understand, we free ourselves and our thoughts from the bondage of the mental chamber and let loose our desires onto the canvas of the world. The next time we become aware that we have a choice about how to communicate, we can opt to use our outside voices and watch their creative powers at work.

❦

TECHNOLOGY AS DISTRACTION
CHOOSING TRUE CONNECTIONS

We are often lured by the promise of new technology to make our lives easier and help connect us to others. While it does so in many ways, it also presents each of us with opportunities to make different choices about how we spend our time and invest our energy. Most gadgets are generally meant to improve the quality of our lives, but it is when we spend too much time with them that they actually do the opposite. By always using our portable e-mailers and cell phones, playing video games, and surfing the Internet, we actually grow less connected and more distracted. In becoming aware of these tendencies, we harness the power to overcome them and make better choices for ourselves and our families.

Once we decide to consciously put our gadgets to work for us, we become masters of our time. We can give our full attention to whatever we are doing and not let phone conversations and other distractions take the place of human contact. Each of us has the ability to consciously choose to be more present in our lives. We can decide at any time to leave our gadgets behind and become aware of the sights and sounds around us in order to expand our awareness and be fully present in our bodies and our surroundings.

When we exercise discernment about how we invest our personal energy, we can be sure that we choose only the best for ourselves and those we love. Our gadgets can be useful tools for our journeys in the material world, but we must not forget that we are spiritual beings having a human experience, and that means interacting with people on a personal level. Choices that enliven us and help us feel connected to our world and our loved ones always deserve our full attention and presence of mind, body, and spirit.

❦

AGREE TO DISAGREE
WORKING THROUGH DIFFERENCES

We all have disagreements. To clash at times with family and friends is a part of life. Whether we simply have a difference of opinion with someone or engage in an argument, disagreements offer us an opportunity to learn and grow.

One of the most important things we can do when we find ourselves in disagreement with others, whether they are close to us or not, is to try to remain calm and be respectful. When we disagree over something minor, we usually just engage in some playful squabbling. However, when we are discussing something of importance to us, or if we take issue with someone we do not particularly like, it may be difficult to keep from becoming angry and exchanging harsh words. From there, it is all too easy for a disagreement to escalate and become a full-blown shouting match.

During any disagreement, it is important to be respectful and let the other person state a dissenting opinion. Then listen and really try to hear what is being said. Try to understand not just the words, but the feelings of the other person as well. Understanding is more important than agreeing. You may not come to an agreement, but you can agree to disagree and still keep the peace.

If a disagreement starts to get heated, take a deep breath and stop talking. Make eye contact, and as difficult as it may be, send the other person love. Try to find compassion. Chances are, there will be an energy shift, and both of you will become calmer and better able to discuss your differences.

We should not, however, withdraw from those close to us when they want to discuss issues. As uncomfortable as conflict may be, when we are able to work through it, the relationship is strengthened. Disagreements offer us a chance to become more accepting, loving people and give others the chance to do the same.

❦

REACHING OUT IN
OUR INSULAR WORLD
MAKING NEW FRIENDS

As we navigate our way through life, we sometimes lose touch with what it is like to have a sense of community. Back when we were young children, certain things—like making friends—were easier. There was no worry about whether somebody liked us . . . it did not matter; we accepted everybody the way they were. There was never judgment—we did not know any different. As adults, we find that our brains sometimes get in the way of our decision-making process with respect to who we want in our sacred circle of friends: that is, our community.

Making new friends as adults can be difficult. Some of us have had friends since elementary school, but as with a lot of things in life, we often grow and move in different directions—and that is okay . . . it is a part of life. But having friends and a sense of community is very important. We all need somebody we can count on; we all want to feel we have a safe place to land.

If you would like to create community in your life, here are some suggestions:

— First you need to get out and about where you can actually meet people—perhaps volunteering somewhere, accepting an invitation to a party that you might not have gone to, or maybe getting acquainted with the folks in your neighborhood. In the 21st century, you can meet people online in community groups. You may be surprised by how many other people out there are looking for new friends, too.

— Next, you need to take action and invite people to be *your* friends. It may sound silly, but most people are very insecure; and if nobody takes the lead, you will be back where you started. So be brave and put yourself out there.

— After you have established your new friendship, it needs upkeep, just like any other relationship. Nurture it, give and take equally, be respectful . . . and let it blossom.

❧⁑☙

10 WAYS TO IMPROVE RELATIONSHIPS
HELPING BONDS THRIVE

1. The relationships you foster will become a mirror of the one you have with yourself. Learn to take responsibility for your own happiness and security and to treat yourself with acceptance, caring, and compassion.

2. Every person desires to be treated lovingly, and simple kindness can often inspire kindness in return. Reflect on those who have made you feel most cared for and appreciated, and emulate them in your interactions with others.

3. Although first impressions highlight similarities, it is often the differences between two people that make a relationship unique. Showing interest in the various cultures, origins, and interests of your friends—whether it be through food, music, or art—can enrich and strengthen your ties.

4. Intimacy cannot thrive without contact. Making time for those important to you, even if it is simply the duration spent writing a letter, demonstrates the depth of your feeling. Try to take a few moments on a regular basis to reach out and make an effort to establish contact.

5. Positive thoughts and deeds inspire love, honesty, and respect. Negativity can only cause stress in relationships. Show others that you are grateful for the bounty with which you have been blessed, and never hesitate to give to others.

6. Share not only the laughter, but the tears as well. In doing so, you will become richer in spirit.

7. Conflict is a natural part of all relationships. Focus on creating a balanced compromise rather than winning or losing an argument. This can draw you and your friend closer together.

8. Feelings of irritation, anger, or frustration flourish when you remain silent. Give voice to your emotions as they arise, using neutral, non-accusatory statements. Make your feelings clear.

9. Being hurt by someone you care for is one of life's great sorrows, but forgiveness is one of its great joys. Practice forgiveness to ease the strain on relationships that have been put to the test—it will bring peace to your soul.

10. You may not know that *you* have changed, although you recognize and may be hurt by changes in others. Find the underlying qualities you appreciate in those you care for, and be tolerant of their evolution, for everything and everyone changes with time.

THE POWER OF UNION
ENTERING INTO PARTNERSHIP

The purpose of partnership is to create something greater than we can create alone—not because of any deficiency or incompleteness in us, but because each of us is unique, with our own talents and abilities, and in partnership we increase the efforts and talents available for creating something meaningful together. All partnerships— whether romantic, creative, or professional—can be catalysts for personal growth. In partnership we harness the power of union.

It is important to choose our partnerships consciously. We may sometimes find ourselves rushing into ones forged quickly during times of need, with perhaps not the clearest intentions. Partnerships created from those starting points might serve our immediate needs, but the repercussions of a union so quickly fostered without much thought can be difficult to recover from. Granted, there is something to learn from every relationship, but looking to another to fix or complete us can turn into a dependent bond. If we can remain clear about what we want and need in a partnership, while staying grounded and remembering that *we* are our own source of happiness and fulfillment, we can create relationships that support and enhance the best of who we are.

Everyone in our lives is a mirror reflecting back the parts we love *and* dislike about ourselves. If we have the courage to recognize our reflections in each other, we can grow through our partnerships. One that offers both acceptance of who we are and an opportunity for personal transformation can be fertile ground for growing a healthy, lasting union. When we find this kind of alliance, we are more likely to want to keep it, invest in it, and nurture it.

Life is a collaborative effort. Much of what we do can be enhanced through partnership. Together, we are stronger because our personal power is multiplied by two. Through partnership, we experience the joys of working, living, and loving together.

❦

PART VI

I recently had a beautiful epiphany as I was lying in bed sick for many days. I was pondering my growing-up years, as I often do, and as I lay there wondering with amazement how I'd survived my childhood, I had the thought: *nature*. I grew up in Seattle, Washington, with the Puget Sound waterway all around and surrounded by two mountain ranges, the Cascades and the Olympics. I was raised on outdoor activities—sailing trips, canoeing, camping, hiking, and the like. For many people this may sound like an ideal life, but as I mentioned, growing up with dysfunction, rage, and mental abuse made it difficult to appreciate even the most wonderful of vacations.

It occurred to me that nature was supporting me, healing me, and helping me survive during each one of those trips. I felt such a connection to the trees, water, rocks, sand,

and mountains. At the time I didn't know I had a gift for connecting with nature and talking with these elements, but I didn't *need* to know . . . I just felt it. It was as if nature was saying, "It's okay. We are with you. We will help you and comfort you."

Almost nothing gives me more pleasure than sitting atop a mountain, looking out at the magnificent display of Mother Earth below me. The smell of being in a forest, the sound of ocean waves, the sun on my face, the wind pushing so hard against my back that it's hard to stand up, watching a bird make a nest in the spring, the scent of the earth just before it starts to rain, a perfectly clear alpine lake left unpolluted . . . when I had this epiphany about nature watching over me, I was so overwhelmed with love for her that I almost couldn't take a breath.

To this very day, if I'm having a hard time or feeling drained, I go outside and connect with nature. I've learned to do this, even if I'm in the middle of a city, just by thinking about the ocean or a mountain in order to make a connection and breathe it in.

⁂

It's common for those who have a deep connection with nature to be devastated by the loss of a pet or animal friend. Losing a beloved animal can break open our hearts so wide that we feel we may never want to allow love in again. Our nonhuman companions love us no matter what we look like, how much money we have, or if we're having a bad day. I love the entire animal kingdom so much that it's often devastating for me to see an animal dead on the side of the road while I'm driving, and I can't watch TV shows or movies with animals that get hurt or die. There have been countless times when I've been meditating, asking the universe to help me with my story ideas for DailyOM, and I've been directed to go outside.

On one particular day, I went out to my deck and found a dead bird—it was a mourning dove. I was heartbroken; I knew I'd been sent outside to find this bird but couldn't figure out why I needed to have this experience. I was then told that it's a great honor to be in the presence of one who is dying or who has died. I pondered this and realized that we always celebrate births, but death isn't talked about, celebrated, or honored—at least not in the U.S. I gave the bird a burial and thanked it for filling my garden with its lovely cooing and giving me so much joy.

Not long after that, I was walking down the street, headed to a restaurant for breakfast, when I witnessed a lot of commotion from an extended family of squirrels. All I could see were these creatures darting about, coming and going in a frenzy, and my heart felt that they were confused and feeling disturbed. When I got closer to the scene, I couldn't believe my eyes: a dead squirrel lay by the side of the road; it had obviously been hit by a car.

The squirrel's tribe was gathered around, sniffing it, nudging it to get up. But the most heart-wrenching part was the sounds the squirrels were making—sounds I'd never heard before, sounds of grief. I stood there crying, not only for the departed squirrel, but for the entire scene that was being played out in front of me. I was so honored to be able to share in this experience with the squirrel tribe, as hard as it was to witness. They were doing what they needed to do to grieve and have closure.

I wasn't done with my lesson yet, and within a month I was to witness another animal death scene at my house. Walking by my French doors, I noticed that a giant bird had landed on the railing of my deck. I had many bird friends that came to visit me and eat from my hand, but this one was the size of a hawk—I later found out that it was a turkey vulture. This is one of the things I loved about living in the hills of Hollywood (I moved to the Los Angeles area as an adult) . . . there was an unbelievable amount of nature present in a city of eight million people. I was immediately drawn to go outside, hoping the bird wouldn't be scared away. He was eating something—and that something turned out to be a little songbird.

My heart was once again crushed: I loved the bird community in my neighborhood, and I was appalled that this bully of a bird had eaten a member of it. I was also very surprised to learn that this particular species did indeed feast upon smaller birds. It was gruesome, but I couldn't *not* look—I was in a trance, and I knew that I was meant to see this, so I sat and watched. The vulture knew that I was there and felt his energy as he ate. He was giving me a gift, and I needed to honor it by being present. All at once I was filled with reverence for nature—the parts we label good and bad, the cycle of birth and death. I cried and gave thanks to this bird for sharing its gift with me.

After this experience, I started to become less angry with the coyotes that ate my cat friends in the neighborhood; after all, they needed to eat and feed their young, too. Although it still makes me terribly sad to witness the death of an animal, I am now able to see the beauty in it as well.

❧

It's hard for me to believe that I spent a good deal of my adult life trying to control nature. I would plant trees and flowers where *I* felt they should go, without giving thought to where *they* would want to be or how their inclusion would affect the other plants in the garden. I've used chemicals and nonorganic means to garden, but now all of that is so far from my current lifestyle that it seems almost foreign. I've come to realize that nature will step up to the plate and meet you if you're willing to listen. I couldn't believe how much of life I'd been missing out on because I'd completely discounted Mother Nature. An entire world existed that I basically ignored and took for granted.

When I lived in Southern California, I spent so much time outside meditating, listening, and observing . . . just *being.* After a while I started to feel the presence of nature—not just her beauty, but her soul. Plants started talking to me. I thought I was crazy. I began to read about nature spirits, and it felt so right to me. It wasn't exactly all fairy tales, after all, and this was so exciting to me. I read books about co-creating *with* nature, whereby I'd sit in my garden and let nature know what vegetable seeds I wanted to plant that season, and she would respond and let *me* know where in the garden they wanted to be planted. I was told what to add to my soil to make it healthy and any other bits of information that would be useful. I'd never tasted such amazing vegetables in my life that first summer I worked with the nature spirits.

I mostly kept this to myself and a few people I trusted, because I was afraid that everyone would think I was nuts. Soon it didn't matter; I didn't care—how could I *not* share this amazing information? I decided I wouldn't preach about it or push it on anybody, but I'd just live it and be my authentic self, and if it interested people, I'd be happy to share my insights with them. As my passion grew, all chemicals left my house; only natural cleaning products were used and only organic food was eaten.

When I started my aromatherapy company in 2000, I used my connection with nature to help me build and develop my product line. I decided which items I wanted to offer, and then I turned to nature for help meditating, "downloading" information about ingredients and how to use the products. The line quickly became very successful, and it was a joy to co-create everything with Mother Nature. Eventually I had to make the decision to let that company go so that I could concentrate on DailyOM and helping people in their personal journeys of life, but I still make products for myself and turn to nature for help whenever possible.

❦

POWER, BEAUTY,
AND WARMTH
KEEPING THE SUN INSIDE

Anyone who has endured a long, dark winter can attest to the power of the sun to both invigorate and relax body, mind, and soul. It can be daunting to begin the months of fall and winter knowing that we may not see as much of the beautiful sun for quite some time. But it is important to remember that even during the darker days of these seasons, the sun is still there shining, as beautiful as ever. Just because it is hidden behind clouds or sets early in our part of the world does not mean that we cannot access its power, beauty, and warmth.

One way to do so is to find a warm spot at home where we can sit or lie down in peace. Closing our eyes, we allow our breath to come and go easily, progressively lengthening each inhale and exhale until we feel very relaxed and peaceful. We imagine that it is a very pleasant summer day and that the sun is shining on us, warming our body.

In particular, we may feel as if a small sun has taken up residence in the area of our solar plexus or our heart. We do not need to think about the location too much and can simply trust our body to let us know where it is.

Spend some time just experiencing this sensation, allowing the heat to radiate from inside your physical self. If you live in a part of the world that loses a lot of light in the winter, you might want to do this exercise each night before retiring. You could also perform it at the beginning of the day, giving yourself a chance to plug into that great source of energy. Keeping the sun inside of you when you are missing it on the outside is a way to say hello to it and let it warm your soul.

WILD WISDOM
ANIMALS AS TEACHERS

Since prehistoric times, animals have acted as companions to humans on their journeys toward enlightenment. There is much we can learn from animals, as they offer us the unique opportunity to transcend the human perspective. Unlike human teachers, they can only impart their wisdom by example, and we learn from them by observation. An animal teacher can be a beloved pet or a creature in the wild. We may even find ourselves noticing them in our own backyards. Even robins and bumblebees have lessons to share.

Animals teach us in a variety of ways about behavior, habit, and instinct. House pets embody an unconditional love that remains unchanged in the face of shape, size, age, race, or gender. They care little for the differences between us and them and simply enjoy loving and being loved. Our pets encourage us to let our guards down, have fun, and take advantage of every opportunity to enjoy life.

You can also learn lessons from the animals you encounter in the wild if you take the time to observe their habits. Cold-blooded animals show adaptability and sensitivity to the environment. Mammals serve as examples of nurturing and playfulness. Animals that live in oceans, lakes, and rivers demonstrate the value of movement and grace. It is even possible to learn from insects that live in highly structured communities in which everyone plays a vital role.

Animals teach you about life, death, survival, sacrifice, and responsibility. If you find yourself drawn to a particular one, ask yourself which of its traits you find most intriguing, and think about how you might mimic those traits. Consider what you might learn from observing the little bird on your windowsill or the mosquito buzzing around a picnic table. Animals express themselves with abandon, freedom, and integrity. It is natural to be drawn to the wisdom offered by your animal teachers, and in accepting it, you discover what is natural and true within *you*.

CHILDREN OF MOTHER NATURE
TREES AND PEOPLE

A tree that is beginning to grow sends roots down into Mother Earth even as it reaches and opens to the sky above, seeking nourishment from the sun and the moisture in the air and in the rain that falls. In the same way, we can envision ourselves as treelike beings, imagining that we have roots reaching down into the earth, energetic strands that keep us connected. At the same time, the crowns of our heads lift to receive nourishment from above. Just like a tree, we seek the sunshine and water we need to survive and thrive. Both trees and people serve as conduits for the intermingling of the opposite and complementary elements of air, water, sun, and earth.

We also share creative ways of growing, regardless of the challenges we come up against in our environments. Trees will even grow through rock, shattering it, in their effort to reach the air and light they need to survive. We are similarly resilient, with a built-in propensity for growth and generating the conditions that promote it. We find creative ways around the obstacles we confront as we move along our paths, gravitating toward the light that feeds us, just as trees grow around other trees and rocks as they make their way upward.

Contemplating the ways in which trees and people mirror one another brings us into alignment with the reality that we are part of Mother Nature. Our children, and the trees and *their* children, will live together on the earth as long as we all survive, sharing the elements and serving jointly to advance nature's plan. Walking in a forest can be a meditation on the interweaving lives of all creatures and the planet on which we all take root and reach for the sky.

❦

BEYOND THE SMALL SELF
BEING A GOOD GLOBAL CITIZEN

It would be difficult to deny that we as a planet are in a very challenging time. Watching or reading the news can be depressing, and we may avoid it because we want and need to keep our energy up to attend to our individual lives.

While there is nothing wrong with knowing when you need a retreat from the news of the day in order to restore your energy, when you *are* restored, remember that the world needs you and your light. The more conscious you are, and the more that consciousness is something you seek, the more power you have to change this planet for the better.

This is why it is important to stay connected with what is going on in the larger world, even when it is difficult and painful and we feel powerless to help. The truth is that bringing our attention to bear on the iniquities on this earth is akin to bringing light into darkness. We can help just by witnessing and sending out loving energy; and further, there are many concrete, positive actions we can take to heal the suffering of the world. Being a good global citizen has to do with how we use our energy—where and how we spend our money, how we think and speak and act, and how we spend our time.

Have a vision for healing the world and a sense of where you fit into manifesting it. And do not hesitate to take action in the direction of that dream. If you have not already, consider choosing a cause that is in alignment with your vision of a beautiful future and support it with any or all of the tools you have: time, money, speech, action.

To keep yourself healthy and vibrant, nurture your connection to a source of energy greater than your small self, knowing that this source will support and heal you as you work to heal the world.

❦⸳ᵒ⸳ᵒᵒ⸳ᵒ⸳❦

WAVES OF HEALING
OCEAN MEDITATION

Like us, the sea is ever changing. And like us, the earth's vast oceans appear at a distance to be stable and homogenous. But beneath the mask of solidity that both we and the sea wear, there lies unpredictability, sensitivity, and power. There is much we can learn from the ocean, representative as it is of our inner landscapes. The rough sounds of its waves are spiritually soothing, and its salt can purify our physical selves. Yet not everyone has the luxury of living by the shore or even visiting the coastlines where water and land meet. The ocean, however, exists in our conscious minds, put there by images we have seen and descriptions we have read. Wherever we are, we can access that mental record and use it as the starting point from which to heal our emotions by meditating on the sea.

To begin, gather together any marine artifacts you may have on hand. Seashells, a vial of sand, beach glass, stones rubbed smooth by the pounding surf, or a recording of ocean sounds can help you slip more deeply into this meditation, but they are not necessary.

Sit quietly and visualize the ocean in your mind's eye. Allow all of your senses to participate in your mental journey. Feel the tiny grains of sand beneath your feet and the cool spray of mist. Hear the sea's rhythmic roar as the waves meet the beach and retreat. Smell the tang of salt in the air. Watch the sun's rays play over the ocean's surface, creating shifting spots of teal, cerulean, cobalt, and green. Don't be surprised if you see dolphins or whales frolicking in the waves—they are there to assist you. Spend a few minutes drinking in the ocean's beauty and appreciating its vast splendor.

Once you are fully engaged with the setting before you, visualize yourself sitting on the beach, facing the ocean and watching the waves advance and retreat. As each new crest of sea water approaches, imagine it carrying healing energy toward you. The magnificent ocean in your thoughts is sending you light and love, while the sun supports your healing efforts and Mother Earth grounds you in the moment so that healing can occur. When you feel you are finished, grant the ocean your earnest gratitude for the aid it has given you. Thank the sun, the sand, and any other elements of your visualization that offered you guidance.

Perform this meditation daily or monthly in order to rid yourself of negativity and reestablish emotional equilibrium. Just as the ocean's tides sweep the shores free of detritus, restoring balance, so can the waves in your mind's eye cleanse your soul of what no longer serves you.

SAYING GOODBYE WITH LOVE
MOURNING THE LOSS OF
AN ANIMAL FRIEND

Animals are amazing. Our pets—whether dogs, cats, lizards, or birds—give us constant companionship, unconditional love, and acceptance without stipulation. They alleviate loneliness and even have the ability to positively affect our health. Because they touch our hearts, when one becomes ill or passes on, it is often as traumatic as the sickness or loss of a family member. And when the unique bond shared by guardian and pet is no longer there, there is an emptiness in the soul that needs to be coped with. Rituals can not only encourage us to constructively deal with loss, but can also ease an ill pet's pain and their transition into the spirit world.

Pets cannot voice their suffering, but it is not difficult to see when they are hurting or no longer enjoying life. Healing touch can induce deep relaxation in an animal while relieving pain and stress. To begin, smooth aromatic oil onto the palms of your hands; then rub them together until you have generated a bundle of healing energy. Place your hands on your pet and stroke its fur, giving it the healing energy you have collected. Concentrate on specific areas of illness, and visualize strength pouring from your hands into your pet.

Healing sessions can be similarly beneficial, and most animals readily accept this gentle treatment. If your pet's condition is terminal, a healing-touch or Reiki session is a good time to talk to your animal companion about the loneliness you will feel when it is gone, as well as the relief that its suffering will be over.

Although society may discourage mourning for pets, the capacity to love an animal brings with it the necessity of a period of grieving. A remembrance such as a photo or special annual plant can bring comfort. If you find yourself unable to let go, you may want to make a candle altar and perform a ceremony of transition. The altar should include four candles, which represent the four directions, and an item that acts as a symbol of your pet. As you light each candle, visualize your pet leaving your side and being taken to the world of spirits. After you have lit the last one, pick up the symbolic item and bid farewell to your beloved animal. Let the candles burn themselves out, and bury the item in a special place.

It may also be helpful to hold a small funeral with friends and family. Although grieving the loss of a cherished pet can take time, rituals can help ease the most important part of dealing with the loss, which is settling your mind and heart and accepting that, in passing, every pet finds its true home.

A MAGICAL POTION
MORNING DEW

The world awakens each day from its nightly slumber, transformed by a sparkling layer of morning dew on the grass, flower petals and leaves, and cars and car windows. These glistening droplets last only a little while, an integral part of what imbues the early morning with its aura of magic. If we sleep too late, we miss the magnificent display of sunlight playing upon an infinite number of tiny crystal balls. To step onto the dew-covered grass is to anoint our feet with a form of water that comes only once a day for a short time, a special gift of the night air that will soon evaporate in the full light of the sun. If we inhale slowly and consciously enough, it is almost as if we are drinking in this magical elixir formed in the boundary between darkness and light.

In one myth, morning dew is believed to be tears from heaven, and in another, the droplets are poured from the vessel of the goddess of dawn. When we see the earth draped with these shimmering drops, it is easy to imagine fairies bathing in the water or a sky god weeping from a longing to be closer to his beloved earth goddess. Witnessing the sparkling beauty of the earth emerging from darkness, we may understand this longing in terms of our own gratitude . . . how blessed we are to be here.

Perhaps heaven really does long to be present on Earth, and perhaps that is why we are here—as conduits between the divine and the earthbound. As we drink the morning dew in with our eyes, our skin, and our breath, it is easy to imagine that it really is a magical potion, a gift from heaven, a reminder of our true purpose, and a daily opportunity to be transformed.

❦⸱⸳✳⸳⸱❦

MYSTERIOUS BEGINNINGS
THE NECESSITY OF WINTER

As any gardener knows, the bulbs that contain the beautiful flowers of spring and summer—daffodils, irises, tulips, and gladioluses—cannot bloom until they have endured a period of cold. Held in the dark earth during the frigid winter months, they undergo internal adjustments and changes invisible to our eyes. Like babies gestating in the lightless, watery wombs of their mothers, they are fully engaged in the process of preparing to be born. So many of the greatest mysteries of life begin in this way, with a powerful urge for growth enclosed in a small, dark space.

We humans have a tendency to yearn for the light, for the arrival of spring, and for the more visible phase of growth that all things express in coming to be. In our love for what we can see with our eyes, we sometimes lose patience for, and interest in, the realm of darkness that nurtures and protects the seeds, bulbs, and babies of the world for such an important part of their life cycles. It is a perilous and mysterious phase of growth, and one that we have little control over; and perhaps that is why we do not celebrate it with quite the same passion that we do the lighter and brighter phases of life. Nevertheless, throughout our lives we ourselves endure similar periods of developing in the darkness.

Meditating on the image of a bulb, seed, or embryo can bring us into alignment with the side of our own natures that is like the earth in winter—seemingly asleep but busily attending to details of growth that create the pattern for the flowers, children, and creative expressions to come. Touching down on this place in ourselves, we may feel at once peaceful and activated, utterly still and yet fully creative, quietly in tune with the dark and mysterious beginnings of life.

MESSENGERS FROM
THE WILDERNESS
WEEDS

Simply expressed, a weed is any plant that grows where it is not wanted. Weeds are defined by their tendency to flourish at the expense of a gardener's overall vision, and we tend to battle their presence in our yards. It is interesting to consider, though, that a plant is a weed only within a certain context, which is to say that one person's weed is another's wildflower. Most of us have pulled at least one dandelion up by its roots and disposed of it in the interest of preserving the look of a perfect green lawn, yet the dandelion is good medicine, packed with healing properties and vitamin-rich leaves that are a delicious, spicy surprise in a summer salad.

In the wild, there is no such thing as a weed because the overall vision is in the hands of Mother Nature, who accommodates and incorporates all forms of life. In nature, balance is achieved over the long term, without the aid—or interference—of a human supervisor. While one plant may prevail over others for a certain period of time, eventually it will reach its peak and then naturally decline, allowing for other forms to be born and survive. This self-regulating realm was the first garden of our ancestors, who learned the art of agriculture from studying the forests and fields of the as-yet-uncultivated earth. In a sense, weeds are vestiges of this wildness, pushing their way into our well-ordered plots, undermining more delicate flora, and flourishing in spite of us.

The next time you see a weed, you might want to look deeply into its roots and discover its name, its habits, and its possible uses. Instead of seeing an unwanted intruder, you might see a healer offering its leaves for a medicinal tea or its flowers for a colorful salad. At the very least, if you look long enough, you will see a messenger from the wilderness of Mother Earth, reminding you that even in the most carefully controlled garden, she cannot be completely ruled out.

❦

ACKNOWLEDGING HISTORY
PERMISSION FROM THE LAND

When we acknowledge that each and every thing on our planet has its own energy and spirit, then we have the opportunity to begin acting from that knowledge. Rather than thinking of rocks and fallen leaves as inanimate objects, we can remember that these items carry the energy of their pasts and their surroundings into the present moment, before becoming something else. Just as we are not truly solid, but molecules in motion, so are all things in the material world. Working in harmony with the universe means acknowledging that we are the same as the land and the stars, that we are all connected, and that we are all in a state of becoming.

It may seem obvious for us to behave with respect and ask permission of an overarching spirit before we enter a sacred place or set foot somewhere with a history that makes us deeply aware of its past. But we can extend that same respect to any area of land. Whether we are merely considering stepping out there for recreation or we have plans for landscaping it, building on it, or moving into an existing structure that occupies it, we can show our respect for all the spirits that have come before us by connecting to the underlying energy. Once we have done that, we can take a moment to ask permission before we move into, remodel, or build in that space.

Beneath the surface of even the smallest plot of land lies years and years of buried history. Each speck of dust, grain of sand, and clod of earth has history that dates from the beginning of time, before it became one of the elements that make up our planet. By thinking before we attempt to claim ownership over the land, we really acknowledge that we can never *truly* own it, but instead hope to work with it to create something new in that space. When we tap into all the energies that make up the land around us, we connect to all who have come before us, and we can be guided by their voices and their ancient wisdom.

❦

KEEPING THINGS IN PERSPECTIVE
MOUNTAINS

Mountains have always captured our imaginations, calling us to scale their heights, to circle and worship at their feet, and to pay homage to their greatness. Mountains are visible from hundreds of miles away, and if we are lucky enough to be on top of one, we can see great stretches of the surrounding earth. As a result, these natural wonders symbolize vision, the ability to rise above the adjacent lowlands and see beyond our immediate vicinity. We are able to witness life from a new perspective—cities and towns that seem so large when we are in them look tiny. We can take the whole thing in with a single glance, regaining our composure and our sense of proportion as we realize how much bigger this world is than we sometimes remember it to be.

Mountains are almost always considered holy and spiritual places, and the energy at the top is undeniably unique. When we are at the summit, it is as if we have ascended to an alternate realm, one in which the air is purer and the energy lighter. Many a human being has climbed to the top of a mountain in order to connect with a higher source of understanding, and many have come back down feeling stronger and wiser. Whenever we are feeling trapped or limited in our vision, a trip to our nearest mountain may be just the cure we need.

There is a reason that "mountain views" are so highly prized in this world, and this is because even from a distance, these ridges and peaks remind us of how small we are, which often comes as a wonderful relief. In addition, mountains illustrate our ability to connect with higher energy. As they rise up from the earth, sometimes disappearing in the clouds that gather around them, they are a visual symbol of earth reaching up into the heavens. Whether we have a mountain view out our window or just see one in a photograph each day, we can rely on these earthly giants to provide inspiration, vision, and a daily reminder of our humble place in the grand scheme of life.

❦

CO-CREATING WITH NATURE
CONSCIOUS GARDENING

Gardens offer us the perfect opportunity to reconnect to our true selves and remember our place in the natural world. Rather than approaching our gardens as mere investments of energy, we can look upon the entire process of gardening—from planting seeds to harvesting food—as a way of deepening our conscious relationship with the creative force of the universe. If we are willing to shift our intention from dominating, or at least directing, nature to co-creating with it instead, we may discover a deep peace and renewed sense of wonder.

To co-create, you must first begin with a foundation of mutual respect. As you cultivate your garden in partnership with nature, you can respect the earth, water, and animals by using organic seeds, soil, and fertilizers. You may also communicate with the plants, insects, and elements involved and create a regular practice of stillness in order to listen for any messages they may have for you. When it comes time for harvesting fresh vegetables or picking beautiful blooms, you might even ask permission first. If you ask with an open heart, you will always receive an answer.

Imagine what it would be like to surrender certain aspects of your human world to the precision and surety of the natural environment. You might decide, for example, to forgo your calendar and plant in rhythm with the cycles of the moon. Or you might choose to ignore clock time and water your garden when the sun hits a certain position in the sky. By opening your garden experience to more of nature's input, you can become available to witness a whole universe of miracles, while engendering a greater sense of honor between the human and natural worlds.

When we recognize ourselves as allies, co-creators with the earth, our relationship to our environment begins to change. We no longer feel the need to control the circumstances around us and can relish the perfection of all that is.

❦

PART VII
GETTING HELP FROM THE UNIVERSE

sking for help—being a receiver rather than a giver—was probably one of the more difficult lessons I had to learn. The universe is set up to be of help to us; there's no wish for us to fail or be unhappy. But we must *ask* for assistance—the system is designed so that when help is asked for, it is given. The tricky part is that sometimes it may not come in the form we imagined or even wanted, and this can create some frustration, for sure.

I find that when this happens to me, I realize that ultimately, the universe had it right all along, looking out for my best interest and helping me in the best way possible for the situation at hand. So many times I found myself wondering why help and answers came in the form they did, and I'd get angry because it wasn't what *I* wanted. I'd think the universe was out to get me, was picking on me, and was having a great big laugh at my expense.

Working with the universe is like any relationship, really: it takes time and practice to understand how to partner together. Eventually you'll come to an understanding, and completely trust that what comes your way is for the very best.

To begin having a relationship with the universe, the best thing you can do is to start a daily practice of meditation and journaling. I usually sit at my altar (although you don't need one) or go outside and ramble with my words for a while to clear my head. I talk about what's bothering me and unload any thoughts that are burdening me. Then I take some deep breaths, relax, and just listen—I'm *still*. When I feel finished, I may reach for my journal and write any thoughts that have come up or any insights received.

This practice can be done at any time of the day and is a great way to begin your new relationship with the universe.

⚜

One of the most common excuses I hear from people when asked why they don't meditate has to be the answer of "I'm too busy." I don't accept this as an excuse for anything—we can all get up ten minutes earlier, watch less TV, or spend less time at our computers or in any of the other distractions we love to indulge in. I too will make the excuse that I have a full day, there's so much to get done, and I just don't have time.

But it is on these days in particular when meditation is exactly what you need to do. I see it as taking vitamins for your soul. Imagine if you left the house completely armed with what you need—you're relaxed, refreshed, clearheaded, and full of energy. This is what meditation can do for you to help you flow through the hectic day ahead, fortified by the energy of the universe. Now imagine leaving the house the way you normally do, stressed-out and late—which way would you prefer to start your day?

When I find myself getting into a pattern of not journaling and meditating, I know something is going on: I'm trying to hide from something, or there's an issue coming to the surface that I don't want to deal with. I let it go on for a while until the realization bonks me over the head to wake me up, and I return to my practice of allowing the universe to help me.

cs✼co

As you begin to work with the universe more, you may find yourself becoming more intuitive and psychic. You'll probably start to have strong thoughts and feelings about people, events, and situations; or you may get quick glimpses of the future. Learning to trust your intuition— like any other gift or skill—can take a lot of practice. When I first started tapping into my intuitive abilities, I'd be given strong, deep-seated feelings about things, but I blew them off and didn't listen, thinking it was just my crazy mind. Events don't have to be big, like avoiding a car accident; they can be as small as getting the feeling you need to move a glass so you don't knock it over.

It's important to always pay attention to intuitive feelings—whether you act on them is your choice, but never discount them. Soon you'll be able to distinguish between an anxious mind and an intuitive feeling, and once you do, this will become an asset in your life. It took me forever to recognize red flags when hiring help, or sometimes I'd recognize one but completely ignore it because I liked the person. It would never take more than a day or so before I realized that I should have paid attention to the bright, waving red-flag signal I received from my intuition about the employee. Similarly, I always know when a car will cut in front of me in traffic—I can feel it before the vehicle even puts on its blinker. Sometimes I think my intuitive thoughts are silly, but I always listen and pay attention.

Listening to your intuition will open up a whole new world for you, and if you continue to pay attention, you can make intuition your lifelong friend. If you ignore it, though, eventually it won't want to come out to play anymore, and it will go back into dormancy until you're ready.

❦

TRUSTING YOUR GUT
LISTENING TO INTUITION

Decisions that you may not be satisfied with can lead you to ask yourself: *How could I have made one choice when my gut feeling pointed to another?*

Because we can look to the past and imagine the future with clarity, there exists a tendency to mull over even minor decisions and to overanalyze people and situations. But when we choose to put aside reasoning processes for just a moment, insights may be revealed.

Listening to your intuitive mind allows you to access a natural cache of wisdom within. By trusting your "gut," you may find that your innate sense of what is right and wrong will become both strong and reliable.

Intuitive or gut-level reactions may seem less credible than decisions based on logic or carefully weighed facts, because intuition is perceived by most as a less intelligent way of coming to conclusions. Every person is naturally intuitive, even if *you* have not learned to tap into this side of yourself. You may also discount your gut feelings, even when they turn out to be right, because you may be afraid of what others will say.

To get in touch with your intuition, first pay attention to sudden perceptions and feelings, even if they are nothing more than a prickling of the hairs on the back of your neck. Acknowledge it, and let go of your fear of being wrong. Trust your inner voice. Keep track of these instances in a journal, and regardless of your decision in each case, determine whether your intuitive feeling was correct. If you already have strong gut feelings, practice acting on them without fear. Do not let doubt keep you from embracing them.

There is no substitute for being prepared, and knowing that you can comfortably trust in your gut feelings can be a vital part of preparedness. With intuition as a tool in your life, it is possible to consider every situation or dilemma in a unique, insightful, and personal way.

SUMMON YOUR ALIVENESS
BEING FULLY PRESENT

When we are fully present, we offer our whole selves to whatever it is that we are doing. Our attention, integrity, and energy are all focused in the moment and on the task at hand. This is a powerful experience, and when we are in this state, we feel completely alive and invigorated. This kind of aliveness comes easily when we are absorbed in work or play that we love, but it is available to us in every moment, and we can learn to summon it regardless of what we are doing. Even tasks or jobs we do not enjoy can become suffused with the light of being present. The more present we are, the more meaningful our entire lives become.

The next time you find yourself fully engaged in the moment—whether you are creating art, trying to solve an interesting puzzle, or talking to your best friend—you may want to take a moment to notice how you feel. You might observe that you are not thinking about what you need to do next, your body is pleasantly humming, or your brain seems tingly. As you enjoy the feeling of being entirely in the present moment, you can resolve to try to recall this sensation later. You might attempt this while driving home or getting ready for bed, allowing yourself to be just as engaged in that experience as you were in the earlier one.

The more we draw ourselves into the present moment, the more we honor the gift of our lives and the people around us. When we are fully present, we give and receive aliveness in equal measure.

For today, try to be fully present in your daily activities and watch a new reality open up for you.

TRANSFORMING
ANGER TO LIGHT
GIVE YOUR ANGER TO THE EARTH

As human beings, we all have anger, at some times more than others. A healthy way of purging it from our bodies is to give it to Mother Earth. We can imagine ourselves being grounded as the electrical energy passes from us into the earth below. We can see it go straight to the core, where it becomes part of the continuous growth process of our planet and is transformed from negative to positive, from dark to light. When we choose to give our anger to the earth, we trust our connection with the natural world we live in and the great universe that fuels it all. Mother Earth will lovingly transform anger into light, so there is no need to feel guilty about unloading it onto her.

We can make this offering of our energy from any location, whether we are many stories up or on a ship at sea. We know that the earth is below us, supporting and sustaining us. If we have the opportunity to physically make contact with it by going outdoors and touching unpaved ground, we may find it easier to connect to nature's energy flow. It may also be easier to receive the stream of positive, calming, healing energy that comes to fill our bodies when we have emptied ourselves of our anger.

To begin, sit and breathe deeply. Ask Mother Earth to accept your anger; and imagine it coming down your spine, out of your tailbone, and into the earth's deep core. To finish, be sure to honor and thank the earth for her loving service.

When we work with our anger in this way, we acknowledge that, like everything else, it is merely energy that can be used positively or negatively. During our grounding meditation, we may be given direction to channel it for its best use. We may find that the earth can help us cleanse misplaced energy so that it can be harnessed for its rightful purpose. When we feel gratitude, we know that we are not misusing the earth for our own selfish purposes. Instead, we are connecting ourselves with the energy of our homeland; and when we do so, we nurture the earth, as it nourishes us.

❦

AVOIDING YOUR TRUE POWER
AFRAID TO MEDITATE

There are times when we feel the pull to meditate but are swayed from it by the excuses that spring to mind. We may think that we are too busy, have no time to ourselves, or lack the right place for this activity. Our minds can think of dozens of reasons to put off meditation. But those are even stronger reasons to look past the illusion of the hustle and bustle of daily life and connect to the place within that intersects with the timeless power and limitless potential of the universe. From that place, we can experience that potent stillness that exists at every moment . . . and it is only as far away as our breath.

It might be useful to ask yourself why you would put off something so beneficial to your peace of mind and general well-being. There may be fear that if you were to slow your frantic pace, your world might fall apart, and then you would have to face the undeniable reality of who you really are and the results of the choices you have made. You might be afraid that you will be forced to make huge changes in order to align yourself with the universe and harness your true potential.

Sometimes the frustrations of the known world seem less scary than the possibilities of the unknown. But the reality is that when we cooperate with the universe by creating our lives from the truth of our being, everything becomes less of a struggle and more of a process of living blissfully on purpose.

Finding yourself alone for a few moments can give you the opportunity to turn within in order to infuse a sense of calm wisdom into your work. Whenever you can take the time to recenter and refocus, it will remind you of how beneficial it is to connect to your source. Then you will make the time for longer sojourns of spirit, because once you are rejuvenated and enlivened by knowing that you are made of energy and light, you can channel this power to create your life in alignment with the highest potential of your soul.

❦

A FULL EMBRACE
EXCLUDING NOTHING
FINDING PEACE WITHIN

Most people agree that a more peaceful world would be the ideal situation for all living creatures. However, we often seem stumped as to how to bring this into being. If we are to have true peace in this world, each one of us must find it in ourselves first. If we do not like ourselves, for example, we probably will not like those around us. If we are in a constant state of inner conflict, then we will probably manifest conflict externally. If we are plagued by fighting within our families, there can be no peace in the world. We must shine the light of inquiry on our internal struggles, because this is the only place we can really create change.

When we initiate the process of looking inside ourselves for the meaning of peace, we will begin to understand why it has always been so difficult to come by. This in itself will enable us to be compassionate toward the many people in the world who find themselves caught up in conflicts, both personal and universal. We may have an experience of peace that we can call up to remind ourselves of what we want to create, but if we are human, we will also feel the pull in the opposite direction—the desire to defend ourselves; to keep what we feel belongs to us; to protect our loved ones, our cherished ideals, and the anger we feel when threatened. This awareness is important because we cannot truly know peace until we understand the many tendencies and passions that endanger our ability to find it. Peace necessarily includes, even as it transcends, all of our primal energy, much of which has been expressed in ways that *contradict* harmony.

Being at peace with ourselves is not about denying or rejecting any part of ourselves. On the contrary, in order to be at peace, we must be willing and able to hold ourselves, in all our complexity, in a full embrace that excludes nothing. This is perhaps the most difficult part for many of us, because we want so much to disown the negative aspects of our humanity. Ironically, though, true peace begins with a willingness to take *responsibility* for our humanity so that we might ultimately transform it in the light of our love.

❦

RIGHT WHERE WE ARE
ENLIGHTENMENT AT HOME

Many spiritual seekers feel called to far-flung places around the globe in the interest of pursuing the path of their enlightenment. This may be the right course of action for certain people, but it is by no means necessary to attain an enlightened consciousness. Enlightenment can take root anywhere on Earth as long as the seeker is an open and ready vessel for higher consciousness. All we need is a powerful intention and a willingness to do the work necessary to move forward on our path.

In terms of spiritual practice, at this moment there are more tools available to more people than at any other time in history. We have access to so much wisdom through the vehicles of books, magazines, the Internet, television, and film. In addition, the time-honored practice of meditation is free; and sitting quietly every day, listening to the universe, is a great way to start the journey within. There is further inspiration in the fact that the greatest teachers we have are our own life experiences, and they come to us daily with new lessons and opportunities to learn. If we look at the people around us, we may realize that we have a spiritual community already intact. If we do not, we can find one—if not in our own neighborhood, then online.

Meanwhile, if we feel called upon to travel in search of teachers and experiences, then by all means, we should. But if we cannot go to India, Burma, or Indonesia, or if we do not have the desire, this is not an obstacle in terms of our spiritual development. In fact, we may simply be aware that our time and energy is best spent in our own homes with our meditation practice and all the complications and joys of our own lives. We can confidently stay in one place, knowing that everything we need to attain enlightenment is always available right where we are.

❦

WORTH THE TIME
MEDITATING MORE WHEN
OUR PLATES ARE FULL

Ironically, when we get busy, the first thing that tends to get cut back is our meditation practice. We have less time and a lot on our plates, so it makes sense that this happens, but in the end it does not really help us. Most of us know from experience that we function much better when we give ourselves time each day to sit in silence. And the more we have to do, the more we need that solitary, quiet time for the day ahead. As a result, while it may sound counterintuitive, it is during busy periods that we need to spend *more* time in meditation rather than less. By being quiet and listening to the universe, we will be given what we need to get through our day.

Expanding our morning meditation by just ten minutes can make a big difference, as can the addition of short meditations to our daily schedule. The truth is, no matter how busy we are, unless we are in the midst of a crisis, we always have five or ten minutes to spare. The key is convincing ourselves that spending that time in meditation is the most fruitful choice. We could be getting the dishes done or heading into work earlier instead, so it is necessary that we come to value the importance of this practice in the context of all the other things competing for attention in our lives. To discover whether it works to meditate more when we are busy, all we have to do is try it.

We can start by creating more time in the morning, either by getting up earlier or by preparing breakfast the night before and using the extra time for meditation. We can also add short meditation breaks into our schedule—five minutes before or after lunch and at night before we go to sleep. When we come from a place of centered calm, we are more effective in handling our busy schedules and more able to keep it all in perspective. If more time in meditation means less time feeling anxious, panicky, and overwhelmed, then it is certainly worth it.

❦

EVERY STEP IS FORWARD
NO GOING BACK

There are times when we feel that we are spinning our wheels in the mud in terms of our spiritual progress. This can be especially true following a period of major growth in which we feel as if we have gained a lot of ground. In fact, this is the way growth goes—periods of intense forward movement give way to periods of what seems like stagnation. In those moments when we feel discouraged, it is helpful to remember that we do not ever really go backward. It may be that we are at a standstill because there is a new obstacle in our path or a new layer to get through, but the hard work we have done cannot be *un*done.

Every step on the path is meaningful, and even one that seems to take us backward is a forward step in the sense that it is what we must do to move to the next level. In addition, an intense growth spurt requires that we rest for a time in order to fully integrate the new energies that have been liberated by our hard work. When we feel we are not making progress, we can encourage ourselves to take a momentary breather. We can meditate more, feed ourselves well, and get extra sleep. Before we know it, we will be spurred on to work toward the next level of our development, and this rest will then make sense as something we needed in order to continue.

Once the sun rises, it does not go backward, but instead follows its path in one direction. It may appear to stand still for a moment in time or to progress more slowly at some point or another, but really it is steadily moving forward. We are the same way, and once we have moved through something, we can never really go back. We may be resting, or revisiting issues that seem old, and it is natural to feel stuck, but in truth we are always taking the next important step forward on our path.

❦

OUTLINING YOUR INTENTIONS
MAKING A LIST OF WHAT YOU WANT

The universe is aware of both the concrete goals we actively pursue and the nebulous dreams we have not yet begun to refine. Neither our struggles nor the daydreams that inspire us are beyond the range of universal perception. Yet to manifest our aspirations, we not only need to know what it is we generally wish to achieve; we also need to clearly articulate these aims to ourselves and the universe. When we create a list of what we want, citing as much detail as possible, our aspirations take on new substance. What was once a mere wish becomes real and achievable when put into words.

As you pour the contents of your heart and soul into your list, your well-defined ambitions become a part of you, and the universe responds to your new determination by placing opportunities related to your objectives in your path. Whatever the nature of your desires, your list can help you channel your intellectual and emotional power into your efforts to realize them.

The list you create should not simply be a record of your individual goals. Rather, it should be a comprehensive, exhaustive catalog of each target you want to reach and your reasons for aiming for it. This may mean that your list will encompass many pages of text, since when you write down and review your ambitions, you empower yourself to more accurately direct your goal-realization efforts. You then also have a framework in place that helps you distinguish success from setbacks.

If you keep your list in a convenient spot and review it daily, you will inadvertently reaffirm your conviction about your aspirations, demonstrating to the universe that you are truly devoted to your chosen path, while keeping your objectives fresh in your mind. If you have an altar, this would be a great place for it.

As you compose your list, try not to edit or judge what you have written. Some of what you want may seem outlandish when considered in the context of your current circumstances. Whether the items on the unique long-term agenda you create are destined to be fulfilled in a year, 10 years, or 20 years, if you are free with your ideas and understand that you may not bring these dreams into the realm of reality for some time, your list will attract the universe's benevolence even as it energizes and inspires you.

ASKING AND RECEIVING
PRAYER AND MEDITATION

Prayer and meditation are similar practices in that they both offer us a connection to the divine, but they also differ from one another in significant ways. Put simply, prayer is when we ask the universe for something, and meditation is when we listen.

When we pray, we use language to express our innermost thoughts and feelings to a higher power. Sometimes we plumb the depths within ourselves and allow whatever comes to the surface to flow out in our prayer. At other times, we pray with words that were written by someone else but which express what we want to say. Prayer is reaching out to the universe with questions, pleas for help, gratitude, and praise.

Meditation, on the other hand, has a silent quality that honors the art of receptivity. When we meditate, we cease movement and allow the activity of our minds and hearts to go on without us, in a sense. Eventually, we fall into a deep silence, a place underlying all the noise and fray of daily human existence. In this place, it becomes possible for us to hear the universe as it speaks for itself, responds to our questions, or sits with us in its silent way.

Both prayer and meditation are indispensable tools for navigating our relationship with the universe and ourselves. They are also natural complements, and one makes way for the other just as the crest of a wave gives way to its hollow. If we tend to do only one—prayer *or* meditation—we may find that we are out of balance, and we might benefit from exploring the missing form of communication. There are times when we need to reach out and express ourselves, fully exorcising our insides, and times when we are empty, ready to rest in quiet receiving. When we allow ourselves to do both, we begin to have a true conversation with the universe.

MAKING THE DECISION
SAYING YES TO THE UNIVERSE

The hardest thing about saying yes to the universe is that it means accepting everything life puts in front of us. Most of us have a habit of going through our days saying no to the things we do not like and yes to the ones we do, yet *everything* we encounter is our life. We may be afraid that if we say yes to the things we do not like, we will be stuck with them forever, but really it is only through acknowledging the existence of what is not working for us that we can begin the process of change. So saying yes does not mean indiscriminately accepting what does not work for us. It means conversing with the universe and starting the conversation with a very powerful word—*yes*.

When we affirm this, we enter into a state of trust that whatever our situation is, we can work with it. We express confidence in ourselves and the universe, and we also express a willingness to learn from whatever comes our way, rather than running and hiding when we do not like what we see. The question we might ask ourselves is what it will take for us to get to the point of saying yes. For some, it takes coming up against something we cannot ignore, escape, or deny—and so we are left no choice but to say yes. For others, it just seems as if a natural progression of events leads us to make the decision to do so.

The first step to saying yes is realizing that in the end it is so much easier than the alternative. Once we understand this, we can begin examining the moments when we resist what is happening and experiment with occasionally yielding instead. It might be scary at first, and even painful at times, but if we continue to say yes to every moment through the process, we will discover the joy of being in a positive conversation with a force much bigger than ourselves.

❦

PART VIII

WORKING WITH ENERGY

Energy is a word that's being used more and more these days, and as it's referenced more in daily life, we seem to have a greater understanding of it. Even a few years back you'd get "the look" from people if you spoke of energy. I occasionally still meet someone who's confused by this word and doesn't have a grasp of what it really means. I like to stay away from science and use real-life events and imagery when describing it.

Have you ever been out and about in a grocery store and somebody walked by you and you had a reaction? This is energy. Maybe you felt scared, a cold shudder went up your spine, or perhaps you had a feeling that you just wanted to talk to this person and get acquainted. This is energy. It doesn't need to be a scientific explanation of electrons and protons; it can be a feeling word . . . just *feel*. When you sense a loving presence in your heart for somebody, this is an exchange of energy. We've all had the experience of walking into a room and "feeling" what was going on. Whether it's happiness or anger or despair, this too is energy.

We have an energy body around our physical one that reflects what we're feeling and thinking inside, and other people with their energy antennae pick up our frequency. Not only do *people* do so, but so does the universe at large. This is why it has become popular recently to be careful with our thoughts and to only think positive ones, because *like* attracts *like*. I believe that this is very valid thinking—that we need to try to stay out of negativity as much as possible. But sometimes we're in a bad mood . . . sometimes our day just isn't going right, and we get mad and think thoughts that may not be in alignment with what we really want.

I developed my own system and technique for dealing with the issue of feeling guilty for not always thinking positive thoughts. I'd just spent nine months basically in bed with a difficult pregnancy, sick and miserable all day, every day. I started feeling sorry for myself because I was so dejected. One day I decided to allow myself to have my pity party for one, but I was going to set a time limit on it. I could have X amount of time, whether it was five minutes or an hour, to cry and feel sorry for myself. Rather than push away and deny my very real feelings, I allowed myself to fully feel my emotions about being sick.

When I was done, I immediately went into a state of gratitude. I was grateful that I had a due date: I knew that in X number of days I'd feel better and no longer be sick. Many people live with chronic pain and illness and don't have the luxury of knowing when it will be over. By crying and having my pity party, I was able to release pent-up negative energy rather than shoving it deeper into my body, where it could later create disease.

Having emotions, feelings, and thoughts is what makes being human so wonderful. Denying what you feel creates energy blockages, and they need to be released. The next time you're feeling bad, experience your emotions and release them. The trick is not to wallow in them and let them *become* you and define who you are. Feel your emotions . . . step into gratitude.

⋘⋙

It's hard for me to think back on my life and realize that I've lived most of it without asking for guidance from the angels. These celestial beings are here to help make our lives easier and are available to serve. I started to call on angels for everything in my life—and then even started to feel guilty that maybe I was hogging all of them! Be assured that there are enough to go around for everybody.

One of the areas where I use their help is to drive, navigate, and find a parking spot. I've assigned a permanent team to my car—angels on the front and back bumpers and one inside to keep me company, especially when I feel panic come on in traffic. Before I drive anywhere for the day, I'll sit in my car and ask that the angels watch over me and protect me from accidents and harm. I can't tell you how many times I probably would have been hit if it weren't for these angels providing a clear buffer.

On one occasion (I was living in Los Angeles at the time), it was one of those rainy days when it pours so hard that the streets flood. I had an appointment 40 minutes away and wasn't looking forward to the commute. But for some reason, on this particular day I decided, or rather I *felt*, that I should put on a big bulky sweater, my little wool booties, and my leather pants, which hadn't been worn for a good ten years at that point. I didn't really question it—I just put the clothes on and prepared to leave. Another odd thing on that day was that I said my prayer to the angels out loud. Usually I'd ask for their help in my head silently, but on this day I found myself doing so with my "outside" voice in front of my altar.

I started my journey, and a few miles from home, I came across a car accident that had already taken place. I saw a woman on the side of the road in obvious distress, and my first reaction was to pull over and help. But I could see that she was being taken care of and there was no need for me to assist. I drove on for 30 minutes, and a few miles from my destination, I had the oddest sensation: it felt as if giant hands were guiding my car along. It was so strange that I found myself checking all of the dashboard indicators, but nothing was wrong. I made a mental note to call my mechanic when I got back home, although I wasn't sure how I was going to explain that it had felt like giant hands were guiding my car!

A mile down the road, I came to a stoplight where I needed to turn right. I looked at the flooded street and decided not to get into the right-hand lane because I didn't want my car to stall. After a few seconds more of surveying, I decided that it couldn't be that deep and proceeded into the turn lane. Just as I put on my blinker and stopped, an accident was happening before my eyes in the intersection—all in slow motion, just as you'd expect. The cars collided and then were locked together in an accident dance and were moving as one . . . directly toward me! I threw the car into reverse and started to back up, but it was too late—I was hit, and hit hard. The first thing that flashed through my mind was that my beautiful car that I'd worked so hard for was going to be totaled, but that feeling quickly left, as I knew I needed to tend to the other drivers. I got out and was thankful I was in my wool booties and leather pants because the water was so deep.

After I helped the other drivers to the nearby gas station, phone calls were made and nerves were calmed. Families and police were spoken to, and my job was over. I went out to survey the damage: My license plate had fallen off—that was it. My car was completely undamaged! I knew then what my morning ritual that day had been about.

The angels had enveloped me in a protective bubble, and the other cars had simply bounced off me. The feeling I had earlier about the giant hands moving me along was the angels getting me to my destination in time to take my place in this event so that I could be of loving, calm assistance to the other drivers.

⋘⋙

If you're like me, you probably have days where you wonder what in the world you're doing on this earth, and maybe you even have those when you don't want to *be* on this planet. I can assure you that these feelings can be quite normal. Most of my life I've spent out of my body—meaning not being fully integrated or grounded in my own physical being. I think a part of me liked being partly in the spirit realm because that's what felt like home to me. None of this was conscious, of course; it was just my coping mechanism for being a supersensitive person in a sometimes harsh reality. I'd often wonder what the point was of being here in a body if I could just be in the spirit world always. Why come to an earth where there is fear, anger, war, and heartache?

As time went on and I became a more aware person, I realized that being in a human body is sometimes the only way that the soul can work things out and experience what it wants to. Our thinking minds may say, *I would never choose to live this life—being sick, poor, in pain, disabled,* and so on. But that is the *thinking* mind, the mind of our bodies. The soul, on the other hand, doesn't think; it just *is,* and it wants to make progress and learn and have experiences to help it grow.

As spirit beings, we can't "act out," as if in a play. We can't feel our emotions, be born, and die. We must have an Earth body to do so. Slowly, as I began to really feel this and learn the lesson that I chose to come to Earth to have particular experiences, it made being here much easier. I know someday I'll go "home" again, and maybe I'll come back and maybe I won't. But that's for my soul to decide, and I'm okay with that.

❦❦❦

BEYOND THE PHYSICAL
WE ARE BEINGS OF LIGHT

We are all beings of light. Put another way, we are spiritual beings having a human experience. As children, most of us know this, but other human beings who have forgotten who they really are, and who cannot help us know ourselves, train us to forget. As a result, we are led to believe that magic is not real, that our invisible playmates do not really exist, and that we are limited beings with only one earthly life to live. There is enormous pressure to conform to this concept of ourselves, so we lose touch with our full potential, forgetting that we are beings of light.

At this time, many of us are reawakening to the truth of who we are because we are living amid such large-scale changes in the world. We need to access this light in order to not only survive but *thrive* as we shift into a new order of consciousness. As the changes around us proceed in rapid succession, we will want to be able to trust our own ability to sense what is happening and how we can best respond.

We are no longer living in a predictable world in which we can trust external authority figures and preexisting ideas about reality to guide us. We need to be able to access the information that will help us navigate these uncertain waters, and the ultimate authority resides in our awareness of ourselves as beings of light.

It is through our connection to this light that we know things beyond what the physical world can tell us and see things beyond what the visible world reveals. In order to access this wisdom, we can simply allow ourselves to remember that we are not limited, as we have been taught. In fact, we are filled with divine grace and power that is ours for the asking. A daily practice of tuning in to this vast potential, conversing with it, and offering ourselves up to it opens the door to reclaiming our true identity, taking ownership of the calling that the time has come to create bliss on Earth.

❦

WHAT WE CANNOT SEE
THE UNSEEN WORLD

Just because we cannot see something does not mean that it does not exist, although this is a common way in which people deny the existence of spirit guides, angels, and other unseen helpers in our lives. However, anyone who has encountered such beings can attest to the fact that they do, indeed, exist . . . just as our breath exists, keeping us alive, even though we cannot see it. The wind exists, too, but we only know this because we feel it on our skin and hear it moving the leaves on the trees. All around us and within us are things we cannot see, yet we know they are just as real as the grass beneath our feet.

What we see and do not see may just be a matter of perspective, like the ladybug who sees the leaf on which she sits but not the tree it grows on or the person sitting on the ground below. And the person beneath the tree may or may not see the ladybug, depending on where he focuses his attention. Still, all of these things—whether seen or not by the person or the ladybug—exist in reality. Some people are more gifted at accessing that which cannot be seen, but given an open and willing heart, anyone can tune in to the invisible realm and begin to find their way.

Human beings have always done this, and it is only recently that we have fallen into distrusting the existence of what we cannot perceive with our eyes. If you have lost touch with the unseen world, all you have to do is resolve to open your heart to its existence and it will make itself known. Closing your eyes in meditation and visualization or engaging the unseen through the written word are just two ways to welcome the invisible back into your life. Whatever you choose to do, cultivating a relationship with that which you cannot see is a time-honored human practice that can greatly enhance your life.

❦

BEING A STRONG CONTAINER
GROUNDING OURSELVES

We often hear people telling us to ground ourselves, but we may not be sure what that means and how we might do it. Grounding ourselves is a way of bringing ourselves literally back to Earth. Some of us are more prone than others to not being firmly rooted in our bodies, essentially leaving them. There is nothing terribly wrong with this, but while we are living on the Earth plane, it is best to stay grounded physically.

One of the easiest ways to ground ourselves is to bring our attention to our breath as it enters and leaves our bodies. After about ten breaths, we will probably find that we feel much more connected to our physical selves. We might then bring our awareness to our bodily sensations, moving from our heads down to our feet, exploring and inquiring. Just a few minutes of this can bring us home to our bodies and to the earth, and this is what it means to ground ourselves.

We can go further by imagining that we have roots growing out of the bottoms of our feet, connecting us to the earth. The roots flow with us, so we can we always move, but at the same time they keep us grounded. We receive powerful energy from the earth, just as we do from the forms of energy we associate with the sky, and the body is a tool that brings these two energies together in a sacred union. When we are grounded, we essentially become a strong container in which our spirits can safely and productively dwell. This is why grounding ourselves every day, especially at the beginning of each, is such a beneficial practice. Fortunately, it is as simple as bringing our conscious awareness to our bodies and the earth on which we walk.

❧

RELATING TO THE NEGATIVE
THE DANGER OF REPRESSION

For the last several years, there has been a lot of focus on the power of positive thinking. Many people have come to misinterpret this wisdom to mean that it is not okay to have a bad mood or a negative thought or feeling. This can lend a kind of superficiality to their relationships with life and with other people. It can also lead them to feel that if a negative thought or feeling comes up, in themselves or someone else, they must immediately block it out. When they do so, they are engaging in the act of repressing a part of themselves that needs to seen, heard, and processed.

When we repress parts of ourselves, they do not go away so much as they get buried deep within us, and they often come out when we least expect it. On the other hand, if we allow ourselves to be fully human—honoring all the thoughts, feelings, and moods that pass through us on a given day—we create a more conscious relationship with ourselves. Instead of blocking out thoughts and feelings that we label as negative, we can simply observe them and then let them go. They only get stuck when we react to them negatively, pushing them down and out of sight, where they get lodged in our unconscious minds. A healthier solution might be to develop a practice of following any negative thought we may have with a positive one. This works well, because positive thoughts are many times more powerful.

Rather than setting our minds up in such a way that we become fearful of the content of our own consciousness, blocking out anything that is less than 100 percent positive, we might resolve to develop a friendlier attitude toward ourselves, trusting in our inherent goodness. When we recognize our true inner worth, a few dark clouds on the horizon of our minds will not intimidate us. We will see them for what they are—small, dark figures passing through an expansive sky of well-being and truth.

REMOVING OBSTRUCTIONS
ALLOWING OUR LIGHT TO SHINE

There are times when we may not feel at our best and brightest. At those times we can take a look at what we might do to let our inner light shine to the fullest. Because we are physical, mental, and spiritual beings, we need to determine where our light is being filtered or blocked. We can work from the outside in, knowing that we are the only ones with the power to dim our radiance, and as we clear away the layers, we can get out of our own way . . . to feel the warmth of our own light shining again.

As vehicles for our minds and spirits, our bodies require proper maintenance. Caring for ourselves is like polishing—helping clear away the accumulation of physical debris that keeps us from operating at our fullest capacity. A simple shift in our thoughts can positively affect our mental state, moving from complaints to gratitude and applying the powerful light of love to any shadowy thoughts. A change of scenery can allow us to see the world in new ways, too.

Once we are free of our restrictions, we can become still and connect to the power at the center of our being. It is always there for us, but when we forget to connect or we siphon our power off in too many directions, we cannot make the most of our energy. Starting from the inside out may direct us to take the right steps for our journeys back to the light, but sometimes it can be difficult to find the stillness if our bodies and minds are in the way. As we practice steps to keep our energy flowing freely and without obstruction, we shine our light brightly, illuminating our own paths and making the world around us glow as well.

❧◈❧

GRACEFUL GUIDANCE
WORKING WITH ANGELS

At some point in our lives, we are likely to find ourselves asking for help—perhaps from no one in particular and without knowing where it could possibly come from. We may have raised our eyes skyward or whispered our need under our breath . . . only to find that somehow we were heard, and the help we needed arrived. It might have come in the form of a person who appeared at the right time; or perhaps it came in the form of luck, chance, or divine intervention. No matter how assistance appears, these are times when we can be sure that there are angels watching over us.

We may find ourselves asking for their help with simple things—like finding a parking spot or watching over loved ones—but then we forget to call on them when we are alone or in pain. We do not have to be aware of them to receive their assistance, but there is comfort in the knowledge that they are there for us when we need them. And when we remain open to their presence, we can call on them whenever we need them, to connect to and be nurtured by their ethereal and heavenly energy.

As symbols of grace and gentle encouragement, angels can offer us comfort as they enfold us in their wings or lift our spirits as they take flight. We may be warmed by their glow, guided by their gentle nudges, or inspired by their whispers in our ears. We may hear the name of our guardian angel and feel a personal connection, but one is not necessary. All that angels need is to be heard, to see us benefit from their guidance, and perhaps to hear a word of thanks directed their way every now and then.

Whether they appear in the guise of a helpful stranger or as a thought that suddenly occurs to us, angels are our loving guides from the unseen realm. With a brush of their angelic wings, they help us make the most of our human experience by balancing it with the spiritual awareness that all things are possible and we are not alone.

❦❧✿❧❦

TENDING YOUR
OWN ENERGY FIELD
FILL YOURSELF FROM THE INSIDE OUT

Life presents us with many opportunities to gain mastery in tending our own energy fields. At times we may want to protect ourselves by using shields of color, light, or angelic presence. Or in order to become more grounded, we may run energy down through our feet or first chakra, rooting ourselves to the earth.

Sometimes it is appropriate to play openly with others in an expansive, flowing state; and at other times, we may want to limit our availability to a chosen few. In certain public environments—such as graduation ceremonies, work conventions, or even weddings—it may be important to remain openhearted and able to connect, while still protecting our individual systems from depletion or overwhelm. In these situations, rather than putting a barrier between ourselves and the world around us, we can fill our energy fields from the inside out. In doing so, we become so filled with our own personal energy that no room is left for outside influences or discordant energy to enter.

When you need to connect with people on a one-to-one basis, separate from the bustling environment around you, here is a visualization technique you might try (you can start in the morning and repeat anytime, as needed): Begin by taking a few moments to breathe deeply and relax. When you are calm and present, envision a ball of light in your solar-plexus area, just above your belly button. Allow it to build there, growing stronger and stronger. Eventually, let it expand throughout the rest of your body until it fills your entire physical and energetic field.

By filling yourself with your own energy in this way, you become fortified with your personal power. You retain access to all of your intuitive and mental abilities. And, you are able to act from a loving space in the midst of any situation.

❦

ETERNALLY PRESENT
PAST-LIFE HEALING

Exploring our past lives is a valuable way to understand ourselves better, and it often leads to healing and the resolution of issues plaguing us in *this* life. However, the key to working with past lives is maintaining an awareness of the current reality in which the present always takes priority. Past lives can be fascinating and entertaining or emotionally seductive, and we can get lost in them, losing touch with the most important thing—the life we are living right now.

Of course, there is a deep connection between our past lives and the present, so it is sometimes hard to say where one begins and the other ends. For example, we may be aware that one of our closest friends or a partner is someone we knew from a past life, and that connection feels like an unbroken cord reaching back in time, reminding us of the vast nature of the soul. We may have issues with this person that stem from the past, or we may just be blessed with a deep love that we are fortunate to have with us *now*. Either way, the issues must be resolved in this life, in the present moment. The love is our gift to experience in this life, not in the past.

In many ways, the gift of dealing with our past lives is the profound revelation of how truly eternal we all are. Once we comprehend this, we can let go of focusing on the details of the past and simply allow our awareness of the eternal to positively influence our ability to be in the moment at hand.

You will know you have received the full fruits of past-life exploration when you find yourself even more powerfully present in the eternal now. The past becomes less distinct as it resolves itself, merging with the present and the future in the nexus of consciousness that holds all time and space. We realize that this moment contains everything within it—the resolved and the unresolved, the past and the future—and that it is from here that we must live our lives.

❦

SPIRITUAL BEING –
PHYSICAL EXPERIENCE
OUR BODIES ON EARTH

We are on this earth, in our physical bodies, because our souls have things to learn that we otherwise could not. It is through our physical selves and the physical world that we can experience life. Purely spiritual beings are just that—they are in a state of *being* rather than *doing,* in a place that is beyond the limitations of time and space. But when we incarnate on the physical plane, we are automatically subject to the laws of physics and the world of dualities. In this place, we grasp what happiness is because we have experienced sadness, and we understand the value and power of light because we have seen darkness. Knowing this, we have the opportunity to let ourselves be spiritual beings having a physical experience.

There is no pain in the spirit realm because we know we are one with the limitless source of the universe. But here, in the material realm, our sense of limitation and separation allows us to feel our emotions and learn about love, forgiveness, and compassion. We go from a spiritual state of oneness to learning how to be in relationships with people who are different and distinct individuals. We come to understand ourselves through our relationships with the world around us—its seasons and landscapes, challenges and opportunities. And through our journey to find our place among so many others, we begin to recognize our own glimmer of light in a constellation of stars.

Once we remember that we are spiritual beings, we can revel in the experience of being human while knowing we are all connected. We can live from the place of oneness, while truly appreciating the beauty of diversity, the bittersweet feeling of love and loss, and the elation of triumph over challenges and adversity. It is through these opposites that we experience life itself, and we can ride through the dark times with the understanding that they will help us to appreciate the light of life and love and spirit more fully. We are here now because we made the choice to have an Earth experience, so now we can choose to enjoy the journey as completely as possible.

❈

INCREASING THE LIGHT
RAISE YOUR VIBRATION

Everything in the universe is made of energy. What differentiates one form from another is the speed at which it vibrates. For example, light vibrates at a very high frequency, and something like a rock does so at a lower one—but at a frequency nonetheless. Human beings also vibrate at different frequencies. Our thoughts and feelings can determine the level at which *we* vibrate, and our vibration goes out into the world and attracts to us energy moving at a similar frequency. This is one of the ways that we create our own reality, which is why we can cause a positive shift in our lives by raising our vibration.

We all know someone we think of as *vibrant*, which literally means "vibrating very rapidly." The people who strike us this way are vibrating at a high frequency, and they can inspire us as we work to raise *our* vibration. On the other hand, we all know people who are very negative or cynical. These people are vibrating at a lower frequency. They can also be an inspiration because they show us where we do not want to be vibrating and why.

To discover where you are in terms of vibrancy, consider the place you fall on a scale between the most pessimistic person you know and the most "vibrant." This is not in order to pass judgment; rather, it is important to know where you are as you begin working to raise your frequency so that you can notice and appreciate your progress.

There are many techniques to raise your vibration, from working with affirmations to visualizing enlightened entities during meditation. One of the most practical ways is to consciously choose where you focus your attention. To understand how powerful this is, take five minutes to describe something you love unreservedly—a person, a movie, an experience, or what have you. When your five minutes are up, you will feel noticeably more positive, and even lighter. If you want to keep raising your vibration, you might commit to spending five minutes every day focusing on the good in your life. As you do so, you will train yourself to be more awake and alive. Over time, you will experience a permanent shift in your vibrancy.

❧

WHOLE-SELF WELL-BEING
HOW THE BODY CLEARS ENERGY

Whole self well-being is, in part, the result of a harmonious flow of energy between our physical and mental selves. When this flow is thrown out of balance for any reason, the body and mind react to one another, rather than *act* cooperatively. Ongoing stress, sadness, anxiety, excitement, and fear can overwhelm the cerebral self, causing traumatic energy to be channeled into the body, which then responds by taking steps to organically dispel the burdening energy and expressing it by means of physical symptoms such as illness, fatigue, or disease. In some cases, these symptoms can simply be allowed to run their natural course, and recovery will come about naturally. In most instances, however, health and wellness can only be restored by a dual course of treatment that acknowledges both the physical manifestations of energy clearing and the underlying emotional causes.

Many of the ailments you experience over the course of your life can be indicative of the body's attempts to process intellectual and emotional energy. Swollen glands, for example, can signal that you are going through a period of emotional cleansing. Even something as simple as a pimple can indicate that your body is ridding itself of toxins and old energy.

In Chinese medicine, intense emotions are held in the body's organs as a matter of course. Grief lurks in the lungs, anger inhabits the liver, fretfulness lingers in the heart, worry is held in the stomach, and the kidneys harbor fright. Coughs or bronchitis can signify that the physical self is clearing away grief, while a loss of appetite may signal that worry is being actively addressed.

When you feel ill or imbalanced, treating your *whole* self rather than the physical self alone can empower you to determine the root cause of sickness. Since you understand that your physical symptoms may be an expression of emotional discomfort, you can establish a balanced treatment regimen to ensure that you quickly recover your good health.

❦⸱⸱⸱❦

THE ART OF FOCUS
ENERGY PROTECTION

Many of us are sensitive to energy, so we make our homes a sanctuary and only leave when we have fully prepared ourselves. We may use gemstones, essential oils, or talismans; or perhaps we call on our angels or surround ourselves in a bubble of light. But we should be conscious of what we are seeking to accomplish. It is important to remember that by shielding ourselves, we might inadvertently keep out the good that is coming our way. All of our tools can be helpful if we use them wisely and keep ourselves engaged in all the world has to offer.

If we instead aim to filter distractions, then we can be like prospectors panning for gold. We learn to filter when we are children as we find out about the world around us. At first every leaf on the ground is a reason to stop and investigate. But as we learn where to focus our attention, the rest becomes background. We do not cut ourselves off from the world; we merely shift our focus.

As humans, we do not always know what is good for us. Sometimes what appears to be a negative situation contains a gem of wisdom that leads to our highest growth. Rather than focusing our thoughts on what we want to keep out of our experience, we may want to turn the light of our attention onto the good we would like to create, while leaving room for something better. By doing so, we allow space for the wisdom of the universe to work its magic on our behalf. If we trust the universe, we know that good is present even if it does not *look* good on the surface. When we shift our focus in this way, we actually attract desired things into our lives, and the rest falls away without the effort of filtering. By practicing the art of focus, we invest our attention and energy into making our lives a positive experience.

PART IX
HELPING OTHERS

I feel I've been truly blessed with all of the life lessons I've been given and have learned from. I have my days when I want to scream "Enough!" but after much digging my heels in the ground, I've come to accept and appreciate all of these lessons.

I've always considered myself a helpful person, willing to give back and assist other people in need, and I'm happy to do this. Somewhere along the way, I started to contribute on a deeper level, more than just writing a check or offering a hug or a smile. I needed to give back to humanity the grace that I'd received from the universe.

I mentioned in the Introduction that I felt it would be almost a waste of life lessons if I were the only one who benefited from everything I had to experience, and an overwhelming desire to help others started to consume me.

It didn't feel like a duty or obligation, and I didn't even think that it was being asked of me; it just felt like the right thing to do, almost like closing the circle or completing the cycle.

⚜

We all know somebody whom everybody turns to for advice, or perhaps *you* are that person—maybe you're everybody's friend and are always the first to volunteer or be helpful. These individuals are thought of as Earth angels—kindhearted, loving, and selfless. I thought *I* was one of those people, until an experience forced me to recognize that my motivation for being helpful wasn't always about the other person, but rather, on a soul level I was really looking to rescue myself. This in itself is not a bad thing at all. Life gives us opportunities to learn and heal at every moment. But it is when we get stuck in helping mode without understanding what our underlying motivation is that we run into trouble.

The most profound example of this for me occurred when I decided to buy a horse. I'd been taking riding lessons for a number of years when I switched barns and was given a lesson horse that was also used as a rental for trail rides. She was the largest member of the herd yet was drastically underweight, as she was not a pack leader and was always pushed away from the feed bin.

It comes as no surprise that I, a person who'd led a life of emotional pain, would be attracted to this horse and immediately want to start helping her. I was told that I could purchase her, and then she could be kept in a private stall and not have to fight for her food or stand out in the mud and rain. I didn't have the money, but then it appeared out of nowhere, and I took that as a sign that I could buy her.

I nursed her back to health, wormed her, gave her anti-biotics for her lung infection, and fed her high-calorie food to put weight on her. In the end, it didn't work out between us, and I had to give her away. I got her healthy, and she gained weight and looked beautiful, which I thought would make her happy, but it didn't. She thought she was being punished by being taken away from her herd, and she started to rebel by bucking me and misbehaving. Daily training did help, but I would have gone broke paying for that kind of help. I sent her to live on a farm out in the countryside, with a young girl and other animals.

After the drama and tears were settled, I realized that my intention for getting involved with my horse was really coming from a place of rescue. My unconscious mind thought that if I could rescue *her*, I would be rescuing a part of myself. I'm grateful for this experience and what it taught me, and now I know that I just need to take a breath first and examine my feelings and what is behind them before making a "rescue."

LOVE SHOWS THE WAY
WE ARE HERE TO SERVE

We are living in a time of great change. Many thinkers and seers agree that humanity and planet Earth are evolving at a quickened pace, and that this evolution will necessarily be severe and seemingly chaotic at times. It is natural for people to react with fear, because these changes will doubtless bring some level of difficulty and loss to many. However, it is essential that we all remember that our souls chose to be here at this time and to be part of this process. Every movement in the universe is one toward love. This is true even in situations that appear on the surface to be the opposite of loving.

Since we chose to be here, we are ready and able to rise to the challenges in which we find ourselves. It is helpful to reflect on our own lives and make any changes necessary to fully support humanity and the planet. When we open our hearts in love instead of closing them in fear, we serve the divine process. We are all powerful spirits who took form at this time in order to serve our fellow humans, our planet, and the universe. As we find ways we can serve, our fear dissipates. We may serve by remaining calm and loving with our children and our families, even as the situation seems dark; by sending money to people who need financial assistance; or by going out into the world and actively helping others rebuild their lives. Regardless of what actions we choose to take, the essential element will be the internal gesture of choosing to remain in love. This is all that is needed.

When it is difficult to remain in love, we may always call upon our unseen helpers: the teachers and guides who are always with us. All we need to do is ask, and then trust that we are being helped. The guidance we receive is love itself, showing us the way.

RECOGNIZING OUR
OWN GREATNESS
THE GREATNESS IN OTHERS

People who possess greatness are said to stand apart from others in some way, usually by the size or originality of their vision and by their ability to manifest it. And yet those who recognize that greatness, whether they display it themselves or not, also have this quality within them; otherwise, they could not see it in another. In many ways, the achievements of one person always belong to many people, for we accomplish nothing alone in this world. Individuals who display greatness rely upon others who are able to see as they do, listen, encourage, and support. Without those people who recognize greatness and move in to support it, even the most exalted ideas, works of art, and political movements would remain unborn.

We are all moved by greatness when we see it, and although the experience is to some degree subjective, we know the feeling of it. When we encounter it, it is as if something in us stirs, awakens, and comes forth to meet what was inside us all along. When we respond to someone else's greatness, we feed our own. We may feel called upon to dedicate ourselves to their vision, or we may be inspired to follow a path we forge ourselves. Either way, we cannot lose when we recognize that the greatness we see in others also belongs to us. Our recognition of this is a call to action that, if heeded, will inspire others to see in us the greatness *they* also possess. This creates a chain reaction unfolding endlessly into the future.

Ultimately, greatness is simply the best of what humanity has to offer. Greatness does what has not been done before and inspires the same courage that it requires. When we see it in others, we know it; and when we trust its presence in ourselves, we embody it.

❦

OFFERING A CONTAINER
HOLDING SPACE FOR OTHERS

We have all been called upon at one time or another to help a loved one through a difficult time. When the help required consists of concrete actions, such as running errands or making phone calls, we know what to do. But sometimes we are called simply to hold space for people as they go through whatever they need to go through. They may need to express anger or grief. They may need to talk or be silent. They may need us to hold their hands or give them time alone. Whatever the case, when we hold space for others, we offer ourselves up as a container for the overwhelming feelings they may be encountering due to their circumstances.

When we offer ourselves in this way, the more centered and grounded we are, the better. Our steadiness allows our companions to lean into us for support, as our presence provides an environment in which they can be free to move. We can also help by being responsive, allowing them to dictate the flow of action from talking to not talking, from anger to grief . . . and back again. By being aware and open, we can help them confront their feelings when that seems right, and back off from them when they need a break. Holding space requires humility, conscientiousness, and the ability to step out of the way, to honestly understand that this is not about us.

When we love someone in this way, we provide a space in which they can simply *be*, feeling what they need to feel without worrying about how they are being perceived. We can provide this offering in person or even from a distance— over the phone or through meditation. However we do it, when we hold space for someone in need, we are bestowing a gift of the highest nature.

SOLACE IN SERVICE
DOING FOR OTHERS

When we feel bad, often our first instinct is to isolate ourselves and focus on what is upsetting us. Sometimes we really do need some downtime, but often the best way to get out of the blues quickly is to turn our attention to other people. In being of service to others, paradoxically we often find answers to our own questions and solutions to our own problems. We also end up feeling more connected to those around us, as well as empowered by the experience of helping someone.

When we reach out to people we can help, we confirm that we are not alone in our own need for support and inspiration, and we also remind ourselves that we are powerful and capable in certain ways. Even as our own problems or moods get the better of us sometimes, there are always others who can use our particular gifts and energy. They, in turn, remind us that we are not the only people in the world with difficulties or issues. We all struggle with the problems of life, and we all feel overwhelmed from time to time, but we can almost always find solace in service.

In an ideal situation, the person we are helping sheds light on our own dilemma, sometimes with a direct piece of advice and sometimes without saying anything at all. Frequently just the act of getting our minds out of the obsessive mode of trying to figure out what to do about our own lives does the trick. Many great inventors and artists have found that the inspiration they need to get to the next level in their creative expression comes not when they are working, but when they are walking around the block or doing dishes. We do ourselves and everyone else a great service when we take a break from our sorrows and extend ourselves to someone in need.

❦❦❦❦❦

ACKNOWLEDGING OUR PAIN
RESCUING THE RESCUER

Some people seem called upon to help others, often from very early on in their childhoods, responding to the needs of family members, strangers, or animals with a selflessness that is impressive. Often these caretakers appear to have very few needs of their own; and the focus of their lives is on rescuing, helping, and healing others. While there are a few people who are truly able to sustain this completely giving lifestyle, the vast majority have needs that lie beneath the surface, unmet and often unseen. In these cases, their motivation to help others may be an extension of a deep desire to heal a wounded part of themselves that is starving for the kind of love and attention they dole out to those around them on a daily basis. For any number of reasons, they are unable to give themselves the love they require, so they give it to others. This does not mean that they are not meant to be helping others, but it does mean that they would do well to turn some of that helping energy within.

One problem with the rescuer model is that these individuals can get stuck in the role, always living in crisis mode at the expense of inner peace and personal growth. Until they resolve their own inner dramas, they play them out in their relationships with others, drawn to those who need them and often unable to acknowledge their own needs or get them met. In the worst-case scenario, they enable other people's dilemmas by not knowing when to stop playing the rescuer and allow them to figure things out on their own. However, if rescuers find the strength to turn within and face the needy aspects of their own psyches, they can become models of empowerment and a true source of healing in the world.

Some signs that you or someone you love may need to rescue the rescuer within are:

- Inner burnout from overgiving
- Underlying resentment
- An inability to admit to having needs of one's own
- An unwillingness to be vulnerable

Help comes when we allow ourselves to admit we need it, acknowledging our humanity and our wholeness by acknowledging our pain. The understanding we gain in the process will naturally inform and inspire our ability to help those in need do the same.

❦

SHARING WISDOM
BECOMING A MENTOR

Most often we think of mentors in terms of successful, professional adults taking disadvantaged youths under their wings, encouraging them to pursue higher education and attain lofty career goals. Yet anyone—old or young, formally educated or street-smart—can be a mentor. We all can, and should, be mentors; and we can mentor anyone, regardless of age, gender, race, or socioeconomic background.

Simply defined, a *mentor* is a wise and trusted person. We all have wisdom to share, and we should feel honored when someone trusts us enough to ask for our guidance. We then have the opportunity to trust in ourselves and our judgment. We come to know that we have the innate good sense to impart our life experience (no matter how long we have lived) and the knowledge we have gained in order to be of value and service to others. We can help them discover themselves and their potential, show them their own brilliance, and guide them in defining and achieving any goals they may have. Mentoring allows us to expose others to new experiences and introduce them to new ideas. In turn, we discover and learn new things about ourselves.

Many of us mentor even when we are not aware we are doing it. The grandmother who teaches a child how to knit is a mentor, for she not only teaches stitches, but she passes on her knowledge of an age-old craft and encourages the next generation to be creative. We may even think of our own children as our mentors, allowing us to view life from the beginning, bringing out our silly side, and showing us how to love unconditionally.

There are many kinds of mentors, and although we may feel intimidated by the responsibility, it is a role we should embrace. We are here on Earth to learn and to pass on life's lessons to others. Whether we mentor someone throughout life with our guidance and counsel, or for just a moment by letting him or her confide in us, we are doing a valuable service. When people reach out, take their hands. They are saying that they trust your wisdom.

❧⚬❁⚬❧

GIVING TO RECEIVE
GENEROSITY

The most difficult time to be generous is when we ourselves are feeling poor. While some of us have experienced actually being in the red financially, there are those of us who would feel broke even if we had a million dollars in the bank. Either way, as the old adage goes, it is always in giving that we receive . . . meaning that when we are living in a state of lack, the gesture we may least want to offer is the very act that could help us create the abundance we seek.

One way to practice generosity is to give energy where it is needed. Donating money to a cause or person in need is one way to do so. Offering attention, love, or a smile to another is an alternative act of giving that we can perform. After all, there are people all over the world who are hungry for love.

Sometimes when we practice generosity, we practice it conditionally. We might be expecting to "receive back" from the person to whom we gave. We might even become angry or resentful if that person does not reciprocate.

However, trust in the natural flow of energy and you will find yourself practicing generosity with no strings attached. This is the purest form of giving. Remember that what you send out will always come back to you. Selflessly help friends in need without expecting them to return the same favor in the same way, and know that you, too, will receive that support from the universe when you need it. Besides, while giving conditionally creates stress (because we are waiting with an invisible balance sheet to receive our due), doing so *un*conditionally generates abundance. We give freely because we trust that there is always an unlimited supply.

Being aware of how much we are always supported by the universe is one of the keys to abundance and generosity. Consciously remember the times you have received support from expected and unexpected sources. Remember anyone who has helped you when you have needed it most, and bless every situation that comes into your life for the lessons and gifts it brings you. Remember that all things given and received emanate from generosity. Giving is an act of gratitude. Plant the seeds of generosity through your acts of giving, and you will grow the fruits of abundance for yourself and those around you.

❦

OWNING THE ROOTS
LEADING BY EXAMPLE

We all know from experience that we cannot change other people, yet most of us have a tendency to try. This is because we naturally feel the need to do something to change situations that we find troubling. It often does not occur to us that the best way to create change is not to try to convince others to change, but to change ourselves. When we make adjustments from within, we become role models for others, and leading by example is much more inspiring than a lecture or an argument.

We sometimes look outside ourselves for what is wrong with the world, but the outside world is really just a mirror reflecting us back to ourselves. When we encounter negativity—anger, depression, or fear—we empower ourselves by looking for its roots inside of ourselves.

For example, if you have a friend who is unreliable, observe yourself and notice if there are ways in which *you* are unreliable. You may be surprised to discover that you have your own struggles with this issue that you were not able to see. Once you own the issue, you can begin to work for change within yourself. This will also enable you to have more compassion for your friend. At the very least, as you strive to be more reliable, you will become more of the person you want to be. In the best-case scenario, you will be an inspiration to others.

You can apply the same method to bigger issues. For example, if there is something you see in the world at large that you would like to change—say, greed—try taking responsibility for changing it in yourself. Instead of being angry with those you see as greedy, seek out the roots of your own greed and come to terms with your power to transform it. This may be the best way to lead the world toward greater moderation and generosity.

LINKS THAT LAST
CREATING COMMUNITY

Since the modern Western lifestyle can isolate us from one another, it is often difficult to forge meaningful connections. Self-protection and mistrust prevent us from approaching neighbors and peers, and we consequently feel as if we do not truly belong anywhere. Yet creating community can be as simple as reaching out within our own neighborhoods. To form the bonds that eventually solidify into long-lasting friendships, we must first be willing to rise above the walls of suspicion and doubt dividing us from the individuals who inhabit our neighborhood, block, or building. We are taught from childhood to fear those we do not know, but community is as much a part of survival as safety. When we take a proactive approach, we can harmoniously unite our neighbors and build a network of support that contributes to the well-being of all involved.

Your overtures of community need not be complicated. If you are new to your neighborhood, sending letters of introduction to your closest neighbors can ensure that their curiosity about you is partly satisfied. Consider telling them a bit about yourself and how you plan to positively contribute to your surroundings, even if it is something as straightforward as planting attractive flowers in your window boxes. Or if others have recently moved in nearby, schedule some time to welcome them to the area. By doing so, you can calm any misgivings they have, while demonstrating that your neighborhood is a nice place to live.

It is much easier to meet people while outdoors, so try to take frequent strolls or sit on your stoop or porch if you have one. Say hello to passersby and you will most likely get to know your neighbors very quickly. And one of the easiest ways to build a sense of community is to organize neighborhood projects and events that bring people together in service or in fun.

Even if you have little in common with your neighbors, your proximity to one another can offer a wonderful opportunity to pursue new friendships and working relationships. You may not see eye to eye on matters of spirituality, politics, or lifestyle, but each of you understands that community helps people feel connected. As you grow to know—and then to like—one another, the city or town you reside in will truly become your home.

❧

IN THE PRESENCE
OF DIFFICULTY
COMPASSION

Compassion is the ability to see the deep connectedness between ourselves and others. Moreover, true compassion recognizes that all the boundaries we perceive between us are an illusion. When we first begin to practice this ideal, this very deep level of understanding may elude us, but we can have faith that if we start where we are, we will eventually feel our way toward it. We move closer every time we see past our own self-concern to accommodate concern for others. And, as with any skill, our compassion grows most in the presence of difficulty.

We practice small acts of compassion every day, when our loved ones are short-tempered or another driver cuts us off in traffic. We extend our forgiveness by trying to understand their point of view; we know how it is to feel stressed-out or irritable.

The practice of compassion becomes more difficult when we find ourselves unable to understand the actions of the person who offends us. These are the situations that ask us to look more deeply into ourselves, into parts of our psyches that we may want to deny, ones that we have repressed because society has labeled them bad or wrong. For example, acts of violence are often well beyond anything we ourselves have perpetrated, so when we are on the receiving end of such acts, we are often at a loss. This is where the real potential for growth begins, because we are called to shine a light inside ourselves and take responsibility for what we have disowned. It is at this juncture that we have the opportunity to transform from within.

This can seem like a very tall order, but when life presents us with circumstances that require our compassion, no matter how difficult it is, we can trust that we are ready. We can call upon all the light we have cultivated so far, allowing it to lead the way into the darkest parts of our own hearts, connecting us to the hearts of others . . . in the understanding that is true compassion.

ornament

WHAT WE ARE MADE OF
CHOOSE LOVE

Love is often presented as the opposite of fear, but true love is not "opposite" anything. It is far more powerful than any negative emotions, as it is the environment in which all things arise. Negative emotions are like sharks swimming in the ocean of love. All things beautiful and fearful, ugly and kind, powerful and small, come into existence, do their thing, and disappear within the context of this great ocean. At the same time, they *are* the very love in which they swim and can never be separated from it. We are made of this love and live our whole lives at one with it, whether we know it or not.

It is only the illusion that we are separate from this great love that causes us to believe that choosing anything *other* than love makes sense or is even possible. In the relative, dualistic world of positive and negative, darkness and light, male and female, we make choices and we learn from them. This is exactly what we are meant to be doing here on Earth. Underlying these relative choices, though, is the choice to be conscious of what we are—which is love—or to be unconscious of it. When we choose the former, we *choose* love. We will still exist in the relative world of opposites and choices and cause and effect, and we will need to make our way here; but doing so with an awareness that we are all made of this love will enable us to be more playful, joyful, loving, and wise. Ultimately, our choices will shed light on the love that makes us all one, enabling those who have forgotten this to return to the source.

The world makes it easy to forget this great love, which is part of why we are here. We are here to remember—and when we forget, to remember again—to choose love.

AFTERWORD

Dear Friends,

I hope that after reading these passages, you've felt inspired to look at your life in a new way. By becoming an active participant in your own life, you'll begin to feel joy like you've never known before. Certainly, you'll continue to have the normal highs and lows that we all encounter on our paths, but now you're stronger and have a spiritual strength that you may not have had before. This is the reward that comes with learning to live.

I'd like to say just one more thing before signing off, and that is to be utterly kind to yourself. Give yourself a break, and be gracious with yourself always. You are a magnificent being of light, and my wish for you is that you shine as brightly as you want to.

Be well,

Madisyn

ABOUT DailyOM

DailyOM features a universal approach to holistic living for the mind, body, and spirit and supports people who want to live a conscious lifestyle. You can find more DailyOM, register for a free daily inspirational newsletter, or take online courses that can help you on your journey of healing and awareness on the DailyOM Website: **www. dailyom.com**.

ABOUT MADISYN TAYLOR

Best-selling author **Madisyn Taylor** is the co-founder and editor-in-chief of the popular inspirational Website DailyOM (**www.dailyom.com**), and she is responsible for all its content. A recognized leader in self-help and New Thought spirituality, she has more than 15 years' experience in personal development and alternative-healing methodologies. When not working, Madisyn can be found meditating in her garden and communing with nature. She lives in Ashland, Oregon, with her husband, Scott Blum, and their son, Oliver.

We hope you enjoyed this Hay House book.
If you'd like to receive our online catalog featuring additional
information on Hay House books and products, or if you'd like
to find out more about the Hay Foundation, please contact:

Hay House, Inc.
P.O. Box 5100
Carlsbad, CA 92018-5100

(760) 431-7695 or **(800) 654-5126**
(760) 431-6948 (fax) or **(800) 650-5115 (fax)**
www.hayhouse.com® • **www.hayfoundation.org**

Published and distributed in Australia by: Hay House Australia Pty.
Ltd., 18/36 Ralph St., Alexandria NSW 2015 • *Phone:* 612-9669-4299
Fax: 612-9669-4144 • www.hayhouse.com.au

Published and distributed in the United Kingdom by: Hay House UK,
Ltd., 292B Kensal Rd., London W10 5BE • *Phone:* 44-20-8962-1230
Fax: 44-20-8962-1239 • www.hayhouse.co.uk

Published and distributed in the Republic of South Africa by:
Hay House SA (Pty), Ltd., P.O. Box 990, Witkoppen 2068 • *Phone/Fax:*
27-11-467-8904 • info@hayhouse.co.za • www.hayhouse.co.za

Published in India by: Hay House Publishers India, Muskaan Complex,
Plot No. 3, B-2, Vasant Kunj, New Delhi 110 070 • *Phone:* 91-11-4176-1620
Fax: 91-11-4176-1630 • www.hayhouse.co.in

Distributed in Canada by: Raincoast, 9050 Shaughnessy St., Vancouver,
B.C. V6P 6E5 • *Phone:* (604) 323-7100 • *Fax:* (604) 323-2600
www.raincoast.com

Take Your Soul on a Vacation

Visit **www.HealYourLife.com®** to regroup, recharge, and reconnect
with your own magnificence. Featuring blogs, mind-body-spirit news,
and life-changing wisdom from Louise Hay and friends.

Visit **www.HealYourLife.com** today!

Mind Your Body,
Mend Your Spirit

Hay House is the ultimate resource for inspirational and health-conscious books, audio programs, movies, events, e-newsletters, member communities, and much more.

Visit **www.hayhouse.com**® today and nourish your soul.

UPLIFTING EVENTS

Join your favorite authors at live events in a city near you or log on to **www.hayhouse.com** to visit with Hay House authors online during live, interactive Web events.

INSPIRATIONAL RADIO

Daily inspiration while you're at work or at home. Enjoy radio programs featuring your favorite authors, streaming live on the Internet 24/7 at **HayHouseRadio.com**®. Tune in and tune up your spirit!

VIP STATUS

Join the Hay House VIP membership program today and enjoy exclusive discounts on books, CDs, calendars, card decks, and more. You'll also receive 10% off all event reservations (excluding cruises). Visit **www.hayhouse.com/wisdom** to join the Hay House Wisdom Community™.

Visit **www.hayhouse.com** and enter priority code 2723
during checkout for special savings!
(One coupon per customer.)